Instant Chromatic Harmonica

The Blues/Jazz Improvisation Method

By David Harp

Book design and layout by Rita Ricketson
Drawings by Don Mayne
Cover Photography by Jay Graham

Distributed by Music Sales Corporation
225 Park Ave. South
New York, NY 10013

Printed in the United States by Vicks Lithograph and Printing Corporation

Dedication

I would like to dedicate this book to all the chromatic players of:

The past — And especially to Little Walter

and George Harmonica Smith

The present — And especially to

Toots Thielemans and Stevie Wonder

And the future — Which just might mean you...

Acknowledgements

I would also like to take this opportunity to thank just a few of the many people who have made this book possible. These good folk include, but are far from limited to:

My partner, Rita, whose patience never fails to amaze me, and my beloved daughter Katie, for her generosity in giving me the time to write, when she would rather be sledding.

My in-laws, Harold, Lillian, and Kenneth Ricketson, whom I should have acknowledged for putting up with me during the writing of my previous three books, last summer.

The Hohner Company, for providing me with the opportunity to purchase dozens of fine chromatics, from eight to sixteen holers, in the past twenty years, and especially for their generous donation of the Super Chromonica model 270 pictured on the cover.

Those chromatic harmonicists who have given me lessons, including Cham Ber Huang, Mark Hummel, and Big Walter Horton.

The great guys at Music Sales — Barrie, Dave Mac, Joey and the rest.

And, lastly, to my parents Fred and Frieda, for providing me with the opportunity to be here to write this. And particularly to my mom, for buying me my first chro in '68, at the long defunct White's Department Store of Massapequa, New York. I remember that day as though it were yesterday, and still wonder — did she *really* know what she was doing?

David Harp

Northern Vermont   Winter, 1991

Contents

The Best Way for *You* to Use this Method

I've designed this chromatic harmonica instructional package so that it can be used by a variety of chromatic harmonica players and would-be chromatic harmonica players. Every reader's needs will be a little bit different. Some of you will need more information on music and blues/jazz theory. Others will already know theory because you've studied another instrument. Some of you will need to learn lots of basic technique, because you've never played any harmonica, while others of you may already play the ten hole harmonica. Some of you may even be good folk or classical chromatic players who just never learned to play blues or jazz.

So study what you need to know, and simply skim over the rest. The descriptions below will help you figure out how to do that, so please see which of the following four categories describes you and your harmonica experience the best. Then I'll describe how each type of chromatic student can best use this method.

Are You a Complete and Total Beginner?

If you've never played *any* type of musical instrument, including the harmonica, you'll need to learn a bit about music in general, and blues/jazz improvisation in particular. You'll also need to study the technique sections, which tell you how to hold the chromatic harmonica, and how to get single notes. In short, you'll pretty much need to read the entire book, although you'll still be able to play right away (especially if you use the box shortcut method described below). But you'll have to continue working on your technique *while* you learn to play the songs and jamms.

It will be easiest for you total beginners to learn using both the tape cassette and the book, so if you have bought the book only, please see my offer on page 111. Having the tape will really help!

Are You a Blues Harmonica Player Who Has Never Tried the Chromatic?

You folks are in for a pleasant surprise, because the chromatic is really easy to play if you can already play blues harp. You'll be able to play the Little Walter style licks and jamms almost instantly! You can use the box method, described below, to skim over the material until you reach the Walter style Draw Jamm Blues on page 36, since you probably won't have any trouble with single noting, rhythm, articulation, or breathing techniques. If anything, they are easier on the chro than on the ten hole! The material that follows the Walter style blues may be challenging (especially learning to use that slide button), but since you already know how the blues should sound, you'll be able to pick out exciting licks pretty quickly!

Are You a Folk or Classical Chro Player Who Wants to Improvise?

If you can already play melodies or classical music on the chromatic, but don't know how to jamm blues or jazz, you're in great shape! You can use the box method, described below, to skim over most of the technique sections (on getting single notes, use of the slide button, and so on) and begin with the Bouncy Blowing Blues and Draw Jamm Blues that follow page 27. If you've never played music with a swing rhythm, be sure to read the section on Swinging The Beat, on page 22. Otherwise, you're ready to blow!

Are You a Musician Who's Never Played the Chromatic?

If you're already a good musician, but have never played the chromatic, you can use the box method to skip over most of the music and improvisational theory parts of the book and just learn the hands-on (mouth-on?) techniques. Then learn my notation system, and you'll be ready to apply your musicianship to an exciting new instrument!

The Box Method

• Information that I consider to be especially important will usually be boxed, like this paragraph. So whenever you see a box, check it out, even if you're just skimming everything else. Checking out all of the boxes throughout the book right now will help to give you a good idea of what's in it, and how to use it.

• Look at all the charts and pictures, too, and at least read each section heading — just to see whether it sounds like you might want to read the rest. Some sections have no box at the end. If the heading for a no-box section sounds interesting, read the entire section. Otherwise, just skip it for now.

• I'll start out as simply as I can, so things may move a bit slowly at first for experienced players. It that's how it feels for *you*, just go from box to box until the material begins to challenge you. Or feel free to read and ponder each word!

Different Strokes for Different Folks

Most of the instructional methods that I create consist of both a book and a recording. Of course, due to customer and retail store expectations, I sometimes have to make the book and cassette available separately, as I do with this one. Depending on your own personal preferences, you may need to use the book part of the method or the tape part more.

Perhaps it would seem obvious that "learning by listening" is the best way to learn to play a musical instrument, but it's not quite as simple as that, since each reader has a different approach to learning. Some of you are visually and analytically oriented, and will want to read each part of this book thoroughly before even considering the purchase of the tape. Others of you may be more audial and less analytical, and will want to listen over and over to the taped instructions, without even cracking the book (unless you're having a problem figuring out which notes are being used in an exercise, and need to look at my notation while you listen).

However, I believe that the clearest, fastest way to learn is with eye and ear coordinated. So I would advise getting both this book and the cassette (the fact that I make more profit when you get both has absolutely nothing to do with this recommendation), and looking at the notation or instructions for each song or exercise in the book *while* you listen to it on the recording. But there's only one expert on your most effective learning method — you! So try to figure out the reading/listening balance that works best for you!

You can use this book with or without the tape. However, if you purchased this book without the cassette, but I've convinced you to buy the tape as well, please see my *Sales Pitch* on page 111 for mail order instructions. If you don't own the tape, you may find that the written licks and songs in the book will be easier to play than the jamming suggestions, which are easier to play when you have recorded background music to play along with.

If You Just Can't Wait...

If you just can't wait to start playing, turn on the cassette (if you have it — and if you're really in a hurry to blow, you should), and glance at the book while you listen. The tape will get you going right away, and you can always come back and read my preliminary sections later on (like when your lips are tired). You'll miss some useful information, but we always pay a price when we're in a hurry! If you've only got the book, well, you'll just have to keep box-reading and skimming until you get to *The Blow Jamm Blues.*

If you absolutely can't wait another minute before playing, turn to page 27, read the section entitled *A Quick Review*, and go on to play some of the simple but satisfying licks and jamms on the pages that follow!

Three Ways to Play Chromatic Harmonica

Gut Players

I believe that there are three general ways of playing blues/jazz style music on the harmonica. Some players are just naturally what I usually call **gut** players. They play from the soul, from deep inside, without needing to think much about what they play. Gut players usually but not always play simpler kinds of blues. They need lots of feeling, but not too much theory. Gut players are more likely to want to learn by listening and doing than by reading or studying. If you're a gut type of player, you'll probably find that the **Little Walter** style of playing appeals to you the most, especially at first.

Eye Players

Some players I like to think of as **eye** players. Eye players often like to play songs that have been written down. They usually prefer to learn a piece by reading it, and then improvise by making slight variations in the piece each time they play it. If you're an eye type of player, you'll probably enjoy playing the melodies and the classic blues and jazz verses that I've written out completely for you, especially at first.

Head Players

Other players are **head** players. Head players usually like to study the music theory that underlies a style of music, then practice the appropriate chords and scales. After learning the chords and scales, head players begin to create variations using those chords and scales. Head players will probably most enjoy the **Toots Thielemans** style of chromatic, and will want to study the theory sections and appendices before playing much.

Combination Players

None of the three types of players listed above are better or worse than the others. I personally believe that learning to **combine** all three ways of relating to music will help you to be the best musician that you can be. If you can learn to play all of my written pieces by eye, then learn all of the scales and chords with your head, and still be able to play from the gut without needing to think about what you've already learned — you'll be in great shape. But that's a tall order, so feel free to experiment with the various styles of playing that I present, and start out by doing what feels rightest. As you become a more accomplished musician, you can then experiment with learning, and combining, the other ways of making music.

Gut players like to play what they feel, **eye** players like to play what's written down, and **head** players like to study theory, then play what they think about. The best players do all three, more or less at once.

How I Gave Up Being a "Musical Idiot" and Learned to Play the Chromatic Harmonica!

I used to consider myself a "musical idiot". I was "tone-deaf", I was "tin-eared", and I "couldn't carry a tune in a bucket". Now I love to play the harmonica (as well as other instruments), and I've taught hundreds of thousands of other "ex-musical idiots" to blow their blues away. If you've always had confidence in your musical abilities, please feel free to skip the rest of this section. If not, then reading about my musical history (or lack thereof) may be encouraging.

As a young child, I enjoyed singing and pretending to play along with records. But a few months of unwanted cello lessons at age 10 discouraged me from trying to make music for years, and convinced me of my 'tone-deafness'. I even took a certain 'macho' pride in being totally unmusical, and liked to joke about it ("I couldn't carry a tune with a handle on it"). However, when my high school friends started a little rock band in 1968, I desperately wanted to be in on the action. Alas, by then everyone believed in my tone-deafness and I was only allowed to carry equipment on stage and drunks off.

By 1969, after my first year in college, I decided to emulate my idol, Bob Dylan, by hitch-hiking to Alaska. I grew a scruffy beard (all I could manage at the time) and bought a denim jacket, but something was missing from my costume...What was it? A harmonica!! And then I hit the road, Jack!

I was able to put my unmusical self-image aside at that time for two reasons. Firstly, the late 1960's were a time of great change for me, so I was able to be somewhat flexible as I traded a 'macho' self-image for a more 'hippie-type' persona. Secondly, hitch-hiking gave me lots of time among people who didn't already 'know' me as 'unmusical' (although some of my first rides quickly noticed my lack of virtuosity, and offered me the choice of shutting up or getting out.)

I'm glad now to say that I kept playing that first day, both during my rides and on the side of the road. After 13 or 14 lip-weary hours I picked out my tune number one, "Blowin' in the Wind", from a Bob Dylan Harp songbook that I bought and brought with me. Being able to play even one song gave me confidence, and more good results followed quickly. The more I played, day by day, the more skillful my lips and ears became, and the better I sounded. And the better I sounded, the more I played. By the time I hit Vancouver, I could play a few songs well enough for my fellow travelers to really enjoy (the first few renditions, anyway).

After a few years of playing for hours every day, I was a fairly decent blues harp player. But I was still intimidated by the idea of playing chromatic harmonica...

The Myth of the Complicated Chromatic

Yes, it is a myth. Although the chromatic looks like it *should* be hard to play, with its slide and double holes, in reality it is easier to play certain styles of music (like Little Walter style blues) on the chro than on the standard diatonic ten hole harp. Unfortunately, when I first bought an inexpensive Chrometta 8, I also purchased an instructional book that required the ability to read standard musical notation. Since I couldn't "read" back then, and the book's directions on how to do so were confusing, I put that Chrometta back in its case, and didn't even look at it for years. When I began to teach blues harp, if a student asked me about chromatic, I spread the standard line: "It's hard to play, and you need to be able to read standard notation. It's not much good for *our* kind of music, anyways..."

In the late 1970's, I attended one of the yearly San Francisco Blues Festivals. As was my habit, I came early with friends, blankets, and picnic baskets to stake out a claim as close to the stage as possible. The late harmonica virtuoso George "Harmonica" Smith was performing, and I could hear him playing wonderful licks in the style of certain of Little Walter's songs. Straining my eyes, I could see that he was playing a large chromatic. And wonder of wonders, he wasn't using the slide — didn't even have a finger on it!

After the concert, I went home and listened to my Little Walter albums. I could now usually tell the songs on which he was using chromatic (the distinctive sound quality was the tip-off), and by applying my knowledge of music theory discovered that he was playing a key of C chromatic in Third Position (more on this, later). I dug out my old Chrometta, and started to play along — without using the slide. To my surprise, it was easy!

I began to listen to more chromatic harmonica music, especially that of Stevie Wonder and Toots Thielemans. This stuff wasn't so easy. I still can't play like Stevie or Toots, but I now know more or less what they're doing, and have begun to create my own style of chro playing.

Blues harmonica players are often scared to try the chromatic, just like I used to be. The myth says that chro is harder than ten hole harp. It's not, especially for blues.

It Really *Isn't* Hard

I know today that playing simplified Little Walter style blues licks on the chromatic is something that anyone can do with *less than an hour* of instruction. I know that anyone can *begin* to learn the more complex styles of Stevie Wonder and Toots Thielemans with just a few more hours of practice. And I've developed an easy way to learn to read standard musical notation, for serious chromaticists. I wish that I had known all these things twenty years ago — if I had, I'd be a great chro player today! But at least I know them now, and teaching you to play feels almost as good to me as playing myself!

For Cassette Users Only

If you have the cassette, start listening it now. It will motivate you, as well as help you to understand the written material. And remember: Feel free to listen to any section over and over — that's what rewind buttons are for!

You may find it useful, if your tape deck has a counter, to write down in this book the counter numbers that correspond to the various sections in the book. Make sure that the tape is rewound all the way, then set the tape counter to zero before you begin. What's the counter number for this section? Why not write it down right here: Counter # _____.

Which Harmonica Should You Use?

Chromatic harmonicas come in a wide range of styles and prices. Eight holers, twelve holers, and sixteen holers are made of plastic, metal, and wood, and range in price from under $30.00 to over $300.00.

As stated on the back cover, you can use any **Key Of C** chromatic harmonica with this package. Readers with 12 and 16 hole chros should also see page 110 in order to get the most out of their instrument.

Warning Note on Koch Brand Harmonicas: Avoid the Koch brand 10 hole Chromonica. It *looks* like a chromatic, but is tuned differently and will not work with this instructional package. It's tuned like a Marine Band, but with a slide button added, so it's missing lots of notes that should be on a chro. If you've got one, give it to a blues harp player you don't much like, and tell them it's a chromatic.

In general, any chro that costs less than $35.00 or so will probably not be a very good instrument. The Chrometta 8 is the least expensive harp that I would recommend buying, but if you think that you're at all serious about playing chro, it's worth shelling out $50.00 or $70.00 for a decent twelve holer.

Chromatic Harmonica Care

- Always rinse your mouth before playing, if you've been eating.

- Don't play it too loudly (for the sake both of harmonica and neighbors).

- Don't keep it in a pocket or purse (unless that pocket is kept absolutely free of lint, change, or other small objects that could get stuck in it). Always keep it in its case (unless you're playing it).

How Your Chromatic Harmonica Works

If you really want to understand how your chromatic harmonica works, you'll need to read my *Music Theory for the Musically Insecure* Appendix, beginning on page 99. It will explain all about notes, sharps (#) and flats (b), octaves and scales. But this is what you really need to know...

Each hole on your chromatic harmonica, whether you have an eight hole, twelve hole, or sixteen hole model, contains four tiny, flexible pieces of metal called **reeds**. Two reeds are on the top of each hole, and two reeds are on the bottom. Each reed is mounted in a

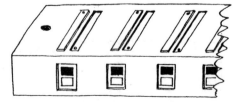

channel that allows air from your mouth to pass around the reed. Air passing around a reed caused that reed to vibrate, and the vibration of the reed is what makes a sound. The sound that one single vibrating reed makes is called a **note**. The sound that two or three neighboring reeds make at the same time is called a **chord**.

On one end of your chro is a **slide button**. When the slide is in its normal **out** position, a slide plate inside the harmonica blocks off the lower half of each hole, and you can only use the two reeds in the upper half of that hole. One of these two reeds will vibrate and produce a note when you **exhale**. The other reed will vibrate and produce a note when you **inhale**.

When you push the **slide in**, the slide plate blocks off the upper half of each hole, and you can only use the two reeds in the lower half of that hole. Just as before, one of these two reeds will vibrate and produce a note when you **exhale**, and the other reed will vibrate and produce a note when you **inhale**.

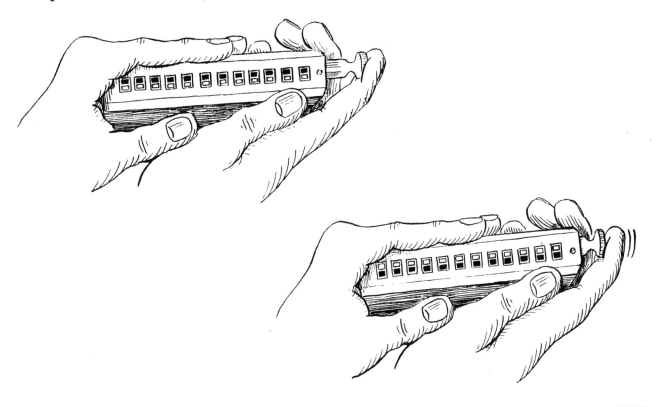

The sound that one single hole makes, either on the inhale or the exhale, is called a **note**. The sound that two or more neighboring holes make is called a **chord**. The button on the side of your chro is called a **slide button**.

Notes on Your Chro

Here is a chart of the notes that are produced by a standard eight holed C chromatic harmonica. As you can see, the notes produced by holes number one through four, and holes number five through eight, are exactly the same (except that the lower numbered notes sound lower).

Notice that each hole produces four notes: one blow note and one draw note when the slide is out, and one blow note and one draw note when the slide is in. As you can see, certain notes are duplicated (like the number two hole draw and the number two hole blow with slide in, both F notes) (or the number four and the number five hole blow with slide either in or out, both C or C# notes).

The fact that there is more than one way to play certain notes is one of the most confusing things about the chromatic. Later on I'll give you an exercise to work with these duplicated notes.

BLOW NOTES UPPER CASE   draw notes lower case

Hole Number	1	2	3	4	5	6	7	8
slide out	Cd	Ef	Ga	bC	Cd	Ef	Ga	bC
slide in	C# d#	F f#	G# a#	cC#	C# d#	F f#	G# a#	cC#

The Big Twelve and Sixteen Hole Chromatics

If you have a **twelve hole model**, holes nine through twelve are exactly the same notes as the one through four or the five through eight holes in the chart above, only higher sounding. There is one exception: The hole twelve draw with slide in is a D note instead of a C. This makes almost no difference to anybody, especially at first.

If you have a **sixteen hole model**, your lowest holes, the one through four with dots over them, will produce exactly the same notes (only lower) as the next four holes, which are also marked one through four, but without dots. Your notes marked one (no dot) through twelve will produce exactly the same notes as a twelve hole model does.

The Chro and the Keyboard

Now look at this chart of the notes produced by a standard piano keyboard. As you can see, all of the "white notes" are notes that can be produced by the key of C chro without using the slide. To obtain the "black notes" (also called "sharp" or # notes and "flat" or b notes) the slide must be pushed in. For more detail on this subject, see page 101.

As I've already mentioned, certain notes can be produced in more than one way. For instance, with the slide pushed in, certain "white notes" (the F and C notes) can be produced, but these notes are also available without using the slide. Knowing about these alternative or doubled notes (and how to get them, both ways) will help you to be a really good chro player, later on.

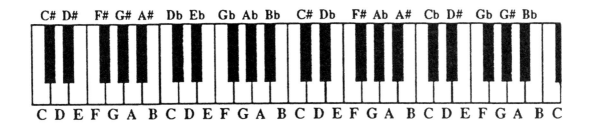

Experiment with your instrument. Place your lips over various holes, and blow out or draw in. Push the slide in while you do this, then release it. Play a note (breathing in or out), then *rapidly* move the slide in and out while you hold the note. Nice effect!

Spend a moment here, if you're a newcomer, and get to know your chro. Check out the note chart to familiarize yourself with the available notes (but don't bother to memorize them, unless you like that kind of thing).

If you can already hold your chro comfortably, and get clear single notes, you can skim or skip the next sections.

Single Notes and Chords

As I've already stated, making a single reed vibrate produces a sound called a **note**. And the only way to make a single reed vibrate is to inhale or exhale through a single hole — a simple thing to write, but not always quite so simple to accomplish, at first.

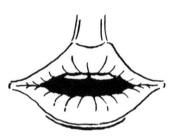

Blowing or drawing through more than one hole at a time makes more than one reed vibrate, and more than one note sound simultaneously. Playing more than one note at a time produces what we call a **chord**, if we are playing notes that sound right together. If not, we produce a discord. Fortunately for us, the chromatic harmonica is built so that we cannot produce discords by accident. Demonstrate this for yourself by placing your lips over a few holes at once, and blow or draw with the slide in or out.

On Single Notes

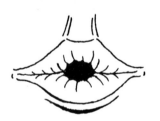

The chords that are available on the chro sound fine, but chromatic harmonica is usually played using single notes. There are two main ways to get them. The **pucker** method simply involves making a small hole with your mouth, as though you were whistling or drinking through a straw, then placing the mouth hole over a single harmonica hole. Begin practicing on hole number one — it's the easiest because there's no hole zero to sneak in on you!

The **tongue blocking** method involves covering four holes with your mouth, and then blocking the three left holes with your tongue. It's harder than puckering, but it allows you to use an advanced technique known as the octave block, later on. If you don't already know how to tongue block, I'd advise you to stick to puckering, for now.

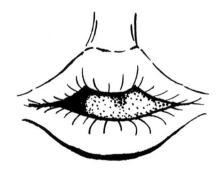

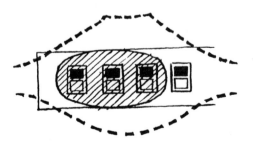

Closing Your Nose

The nose is not normally used in playing the harmonica, although I occasionally play through a nostril to amuse young children, or to discourage inebriated would-be harmonicists at parties from borrowing my instrument. So practice a moment of breathing through your mouth only, with your nose shut. If you're not sure how to do that, just think of blowing out the candles on a birthday cake, or drinking a thick milkshake with a straw. In both cases, you would prevent air from escaping through your nose by tightening certain muscles (collectively referred to as the soft palate) in the upper back part of your mouth.

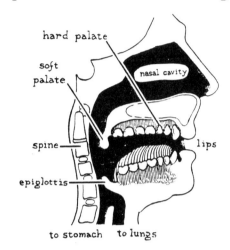

If you can't play one single hole at a time, you can go on — but keep working on it. Getting single notes is important!

How to Hold Your Chro

Most chro players push the left end (that's the low numbered end, opposite the slide end) of their instrument into the web between the thumb and forefinger of their left hand. Then they use their right forefinger to work the slide button. The fingers of the left hand should be kept together so that they don't wander down to block the sound as it comes out of the harmonica.

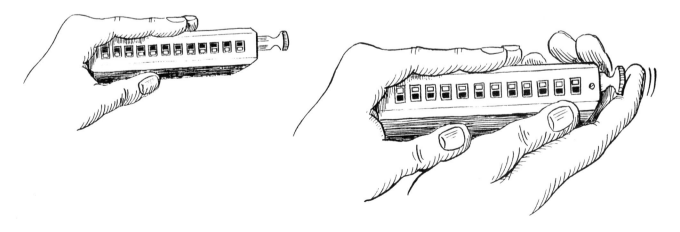

For the special tone effect known as the **hand wah wah**, you must form a cup on the side of the harmonica away from your mouth. Do this as pictured, if you can. Practice by looking in the mirror, to make sure that your hands form a seal. If you have a large chro and small hands, this can be quite difficult. Don't worry about it too much.

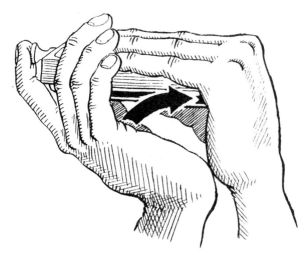

If you aren't trying to cup the harp, you can hold your right hand in any way that's comfortable, so long as your right forefinger stays on the button. I usually keep my right thumb near my left, and use it to support the instrument. Then it's reasonably convenient to shift into a cupped position by bringing the heel of my right hand over to but against my left hand.

For single hand playing, I sometimes have the bad but convenient habit of holding my harp in my right hand, with palm on bottom, fingers on top, and thumb working the slide button. But it is probably better to single hand it as pictured below, with thumb supporting the harmonica from beneath, fingers balancing from the top, and right forefinger working the slide. This way, you keep your forefinger in shape, instead of confusing things by using your thumb.

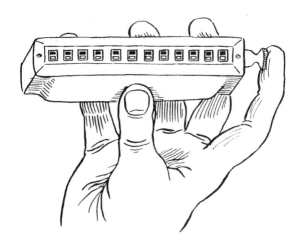

We've Got Rhythm

There's really only one more thing you need to know about before you begin jamming: Rhythm! If you think that you've got good rhythm, you can skim the next sections, and just practice saying the rhythm patterns below while tapping your foot.

If you've always had problems "keeping a beat", help is on the way, in the form of the following instructions! A hint to the rhythmically insecure: If you really have a hard time, the cassette will be of more value to you than the book. And check out my new *Instant Rhythm Kit* offer, on page 111.

Developing Rhythm

If you've ever tapped your foot while listening to your favorite band, you already understand how a **beat** is the pulse that underlies a piece of music. **Rhythm** might be defined as the way in which we break that beat into even smaller parts.

Blues music is often divided into four beat units called **measures** or **bars**, so it's important to practice counting out bars. Try tapping your foot (once for each number) while you say:

One Two Three Four   **One** Two Three Four

Emphasize each "one" by saying it louder, and try to make sure that each foot tap takes the exact same amount of time as the rest. If this seems hard, try doing it while you walk. And observe each foot tap closely — you'll notice something interesting.

Each beat is composed of two parts. The **downbeat** occurs exactly as your foot hits the floor. The **upbeat** is the time that passes between downbeats.

My notation system uses a dot • to indicate exactly where the downbeat falls, that is, exactly when your foot should hit the floor.

•	•	•	•	•	•	•	•
one	two	three	four	one	two	three	four

Instead of simply counting, try *saying* the following two bar (eight beat) phrase. It's best to whisper it forcefully rather than saying it in a normal voice, since that's how you'll be using it later on, as I'll describe in detail soon.

Notice the **countoff** ("one two three four") before the actual phrase begins. The countoff helps a musician to establish a steady beat before beginning to play. From now on, say your countoff before beginning to say or play any piece of music that has timing dots written over it, even though I won't be writing them out (for space reasons). It's a good habit for all players to have. Occasionally a piece will begin with a "one two three" countoff, but if that's the case, I'll warn you beforehand.

• • • • • • • • • • • •

one two three four   **Dir-ty   Dir-ty   Dog   Dir-ty   Dir-ty   Dog**

Notice how the "Dir" happens just as your foot hits the floor, and the "ty" happens while your foot is rising up between taps. There is also one tap that could be called a **"beat of silence"**, after each "Dog". Each three word phrase with its beat of silence forms one single four beat bar. Beats of silence are convenient times to breathe — take advantage of them, and take a breath!

Swinging the Beat

Blues musicians often like to emphasize the downbeats, by playing them longer and louder than the upbeats. This is called **swinging** the beat. It can also be called a **blues shuffle** beat.

If we really want to be exact, in a swing beat we usually hold the downbeat for twice as long (two thirds of a beat) as the upbeat (one third of a beat). And in a blues shuffle we usually hold the downbeat three times as long (three quarters of a beat) as the upbeat (one quarter of a beat). But that's pretty advanced rhythm work, so I won't go into it here, since it's covered in the *Instant Rhythm Kit*.

Now say some swingin' Dirty Dogs by saying the "dir" parts louder and holding them a touch longer than the "ty" parts, which will be short and slurred-over (like "da"). I'll illustrate this on the cassette, natch.

• • • • • • • •

dirr-da **dirr-**da **dog**   **dirr-**da **dirr-**da **dog**

...er by *hearing* about it than by *reading* about it. So ...orded section on rhythm, a few times if necessary. ...' Dogs", you've got rhythm!

...e that you see notated (like the Dirty Dirty Dog ...lerstand, reading the next box below it *may* help. ...re to break down and read the entire section, or ...'ve got one.

... tongue and the roof of your mouth, and say the syllable "D... ...o it again, more forcefully. You'll probably notice that you begin with your nose shut, and the tip of your tongue pushed up against the roof of your mouth. Air pressure builds up behind your tongue. Then suddenly your tongue drops, and the "Da" rushes out like a dam bursting.

Now try saying "Ta". Feels almost the same as "Da", right? But "Ka" feels different, because you're raising the back of the tongue to block the air flow, instead of the tip. Say "Tuka", and observe the use of both the tip and the back of your tongue. **Whisper** these nonsense syllables a few more times, and notice that the tongue movements are exactly the same, whether you are whispering them or saying them out loud.

Using the tongue to break up the flow of air through the mouth is called **articulation**. It's one of the most important techniques used to create rhythms, so spend a moment now practicing the following articulation rhythms.

"Dirty Dirty Dog" should be familiar by now. Feel free to substitute other syllables if you prefer (or if you feel funny saying the Dirty Dogs out loud). "Dada Dada Da" works just as well, if you keep the same rhythm as the dirty dogs. Don't leave out the beat of silence in each of the two following four beat (one bar) rhythms!

Say each of the following rhythms out loud, then whisper them forcefully through your chro. Swing 'em! Don't worry about which holes you're whispering through — the 4 and 5 work fine, but feel free to experiment!

•	•	•	•		•	•	•	•
Dirty	**Dirty**	**Dog**			**Dada**	**Dada**	**Da**	

Here's an eight beat (or two bar) rhythm pattern, with three beats of silence. Once again, use "Da" and "Dada" or "Ta" and "Tata" instead of Dirty and Dog, if you like. I'll be using these syllables interchangeably from now on.

·   ·   ·   ·   ·   · · ·

Dirty   Dirty   Ding   Dong   Dog

·   ·   ·   ·   ·   · · ·

Dada   Dada   Da   Da   Da

You can create a 16 beat (four bar) rhythm pattern by combining two of the four beat patterns with one eight beat pattern, like this:

·   ·   ·   ·   ·   ·   ·   ·

Dirty   Dirty   Dog   Dada   Dada   Da

·   ·   ·   ·   ·   · · ·

Dirty   Dirty   Ding   Dong   Dog

Say the above four bar pattern a few times. Of course it feels a bit funny! On the tape, I'll play a few seconds of rhythm track, so that you can feel the beat. Then I'll say "one two three GO!", and you can start articulating along with the background music. If you are not using the tape, just practice saying these articulations. Here's a 16 beat variation on the one we just did, which also features a phrase that begins on an upbeat (notice that the "da" occurs between beats):

·   ·   ·   ·   ·   ·   ·   ·

Dog   Dog   Dirty   Da Dog   Dog   Dirty

·   ·   ·   ·   ·   · · ·

Dog   Dog   Dirty   Dog   Dog

Here's another 16 beater, once more made up of two four beaters (including one bar that has a beat of silence in its *middle*) plus an eight beater:

·   ·   ·   ·   ·   ·   ·   ·

Dirty   Dog   Dog   Dirty   Dog

·   ·   ·   ·   ·   · · ·

Dirty   Dirty   Dirty   Dog

Now you can do either of two things. Take the four and eight beat rhythm patterns that I've given you, and put them together in various combinations. Or else make up some four, eight, or sixteen beat rhythm patterns of your own.

Blues rhythm patterns are usually four, eight, or sixteen beats long, and are divided into four beat units called **bars**. Practice playing lots of bars of sound. Just go back and use your tongue to break up your breath by whispering the various articulation patterns above through your chromatic. For now, simply choose any one or two holes (like the 4 and 5 holes, blowing out) to whisper through.

HarpTab™

It's time to start playing some more complex combinations of notes now, so I need to be able to describe which notes to use.

HarpTab™, short for Harmonica Tablature Notation System, is my simple way of writing down harmonica music. It tells you which hole or holes to breathe in or out on, and for how long. Later on, I'll use it to tell you when to push in the slide button. Harptab™ works like this:

- Numbers refer to the hole numbers on top of your harmonica.

- I means **breathe In**.

- O means **breathe Out**.

- **Dots** • represent **downbeats**, and tell you **how long to hold a note**.

For example: <u>4</u> means breathe out on the hole marked 4.
         O

And <u>**6**</u> means breathe in on the hole marked 6.
   I

• If **two or more holes are supposed to be played together** (as a chord) they will be **underlined.**

For Example: **4 5** means breathe out on holes number 4 and 5.

               O

If I need to describe a note while writing a line like this, I'll put the In or Out **next to** the numerical hole number, not under it. So **4 5 Out** would mean breathe out on holes number four and five, and **5 In** would mean breathe in on hole number five.

Where the Heck Is Hole Number Seven (or Eight, or Three)?

None of the music that you're going to play now requires the use of single notes. For that reason, it isn't too important, yet, to be able to find any specific hole. Later on, it will be. For now, just kind of generally **aim** at the holes you want, high end, low end, or middle.

If you need a bit more help with this, here are a few tips on locating whichever hole you want to play. They might help you do the next exercise. Soon, you won't need tricks like these, because the more you play, the easier it gets to find your way around on the old "ten holer".

For some, the temptation is to try to locate a particular hole by keeping your eyes on the little numbers on the cover plate. This will rapidly make you cross-eyed, however, since as the harp approaches your mouth you can no longer see the numbers. So let's forget about that method right now!

Fortunately, the mouth is one of the most sensitive and quick-learning organs of the body. This is due to the fact that a large portion of the brain is devoted to operating the mouth (although hearing certain people talk may make you wonder about that). So your lips will quickly learn exactly where every hole is, often a few hours of playing.

At first, however, you may need to "count holes" from the left with your tongue-tip ("un, oo, ee, or...") to make sure that you are on the desired hole. Or you can place a particular hole in your mouth by centering your forefinger over the hole you want before placing it to your lips. Then just touch your forefinger to the center of your upper lip and presto! There you are!

If you have trouble finding the notes to use in the following exercise, check out the two little tricks above. They'll help.

Bouncy Blowin' Blues Jamm In C

Ready for your first Jamm Session? I hope so, because it's time to go for it! You've already learned everything you need to know to create some simple sounds of your own, or even to play along with some keyboard music. Our jamm will sound more happy and bouncy than bluesy, but that's okay for now. We'll get down home and funky in our *next* jamm session!

Why It Works

Our Bouncy Blowin' Blues Jamm in C works because all of the Out notes on the chromatic (without using the slide button) are notes that form the C Major Chord. And the background music for this jamm is composed exclusively of C Major Chord notes. But for now, all you really need to know is that it works! Do it!

A Quick Review

- Put your mouth over holes four and five

- Your upper and lower front teeth should be no more than a quarter inch apart. They should be almost, but not quite touching the front of the harp.

- Put the harmonica well in between your lips.

- Start out with a good lungful of air, and keep your **nose shut**.

- Blow out, using your tongue to **whisper** (don't say it out loud) the following Dirty Dirty Dog type pattern. **Remember, O means breathe Out, and a dot without anything under it is a beat of silence!**

Catch a quick inhaled breath during the beat of silence, by opening your mouth while keeping the harmonica firmly pressed into position against your upper lip. This lets you breathe *silently* around the harmonica instead of through it.

•	•	•	•		•	•	•	•
Dirty	**Dirty**	**Dog**			**Dada**	**Dada**	**Da**	
<u>45</u>	<u>45</u>	<u>45</u>			<u>45</u>	<u>45</u>	<u>45</u>	
Out	**Out**	**Out**			**O**	**O**	**O**	

If you have the cassette, play the Dirty Dog pattern along with my keyboard backing, just as I do on the tape. Stay on the 4 and 5 Out, and articulate some of the other rhythm patterns from page 24. If you don't have the tape, continue to practice the following licks, and read the section entitled *Jamming Without The Tape*, below.

Movin' the C Jamm Around

All of the Out notes (which happen to be, on a C harmonica, the notes of a C chord) will sound just fine when played together, or when played along with the C keyboard play-along backing. You can play **any Out notes**, in any combination — you just can't go wrong! Following are a few ideas and techniques that will help you to create your own improvisations, as well as a few **licks** that I like to use.

Licks and Riffs

Licks (also called **riffs**) are note combinations that you memorize, so that you can use them in appropriate places without having to think much. They're a bit like cliches, or favorite expressions which become part of your verbal bag of tricks. You can create licks of your own (we'll learn lots more about that, later), or memorize mine, or both. As you get to know your instrument better, you will be able to learn licks from records and tapes.

Your First Lick

Let's start by moving the harmonica just a little bit, for the Up and Down Dirty Dirty Dog Lick, as it is popularly known by me.

Begin on holes number five and six. **Make sure that your lips are wet, so that the harmonica *slides* rather than pulls.** Move up to holes five and six for the first "Dog", then down to holes number three and four for the second, as notated below:

•	•	•	•	•	•	•	•
Dirty	Dirty	Dog		Dada	Dada	Da	
56	56	67		56	56	34	
Out	Out	Out		O	O	O	

Learning the Distance Between Holes

At first, it's hard to tell how far to move the harmonica to go from one hole to the next. It's easy to accidentally stay on the original hole (that is, not move far enough) or to end up two holes away (move too much).

The actual distance between holes is about 3/8 of an inch, for all the good that knowing it will do you. It's just a matter of practice. Listen to my demonstrations, and spend just one or two minutes a day practicing the taped distance exercise. You'll get it *eventually*, and you don't *really* need it now!

More Super Easy Licks

Try a 16 beat Up and Down Dog lick like this one:

•	•	•	•	•	•	•	•
Dirty	Dirty	Dog		Dada	Dada	Da	
56	56	67		56	56	34	
Out	Out	Out		O	O	O	

•	•	•	•	•	•	•	•
Dirty	Dirty	Ding	Dong	Dog			
56	56	67	67	56			
Out	Out	Out	O	O			

And here's another 16 beater, the Low to High Dog lick. Don't worry much about being on exactly the notes I've written, as I've just notated this one to give you some reading practice. Just generally go from low to high. Make absolutely sure that your lips are wet for this one!

•	•	•	•		•	•	•	•
Dirty	**Dirty**	**Dog**			**Dada**	**Dada**	**Da**	
<u>12</u>	<u>23</u>	<u>34</u>			<u>34</u>	<u>45</u>	<u>56</u>	
Out	Out	Out			O	O	O	

•	•	•	•	•		• • •
Dirty	**Dirty**	**Ding**	**Dong**	**Dog**		
<u>56</u>	<u>67</u>	<u>78</u>	<u>78</u>	<u>45</u>		
Out	O	O	O	O		

Get the idea? Try the High to Low Dog lick now, by starting around the high end of your chro and working your way down to the low end. And try a Low to Middle Then Back to Low Dog lick as well. Just use the rhythm articulation patterns that you learned, and move up and down the harp — it's easy!

Make up some more licks yourself, using the other rhythm patterns from pages 22 and 24 with a variety of high, middle and low Out notes. Or make up some rhythms of your own, and blow 'em out anywhere through your harmonica!

Gliding Around

With your lips well wetted, glide from one end to the other, from high to low, and from low to high. Try the Dirty Dog Slide lick: start low, glide up to the middle of your chro on the "Dir" syllable, and back down to the low end on the "ty". Do the same thing again for the second Dirty, then just glide from low to middle for the final Dog. Now try doing the same motions again, but going from the middle of the harp to the high end.

•					•					•		
D	**i**	**r**	**t**	**y**	**D**	**i**	**r**	**t**	**y**	**D**	**o**	**g**
1	2 3 4 5 4 3 2 1				1	2 3 4 5 4 3 2 1				1 2 3 4 5		

All Out Notes

When gliding, you can either hold your head still, and move your harmonica, or hold your harmonica steady and move your head. Works perfectly well either way.

The Jump

Instead of gliding smoothly from note to note, we can also cover long distances on the harmonica by jumping from place to place. Try jumping back and forth from the lowest hole to the highest, then back, or any other distances. Remember, in this example, use only Out notes:

•	•	•	•	•	•	•	•
Dir-ty	**Dir-ty**	**Dog**		**Da-da**	**Da-da**	**Da**	
low-hi	low-hi	low		low-hi	low-hi	low	

•	•	•	•	•	• • •
Dir-ty	**Dir-ty**	**Ding**	**Dong**	**Dog**	
low-hi	low-hi	low	high	low	

Putting It All Together

Wet your lips and gliiiide around in the Dirty Dog (or any other) rhythm. Turn the lights down low and the tape (if you've got it) up high, and listen to my examples of licks, glides, and jumps. Or just close your eyes, open your mind, and jamm some yourself!

Use some of the hints, tricks, and licks above, or make up your own. As long as you stick to the OUT notes, you literally can't go wrong!

Jamming Without The Tape

If you don't have the tape, but would still like to jamm along with something, please turn to the Accompaniment Appendix on page 109.

More Stuff You Can Play Right Away

If you've made it this far, you're ready to play the songs on pages 60 to 65. I put them further along in the book because they illustrate certain things about music theory that I'd like you to know, but you sure don't need to know the theory to enjoy playing the songs. So if you feel like taking a quick break from the blues, give 'em a try. Just remember that "I" means breathe **In**, "O" means **Out**, and you've got it made!

About the Boxes

The boxes will be few and far between from now on. That's because you are now into some pretty meaty stuff, and from here on I'll let *you* choose what's important (and satisfying). Once you've covered the Draw Blues below, you can go straight to some *Little Walter* style chro (page 36), some *12 Bar Blues* (page 50), or begin working on your *Toots* type chops with the arpeggiated chords (page 54) and C Blues Scale (page 84).

About Wooziness

Some people feel light-headed when they first begin to play, due to excess oxygen passing through the lungs. If this happens, you can either stop playing for a moment, play more softly (which uses less air), or sit down and keep playing. Eventually you'll get used to the increased air flow, and the wooziness will only occur if you play *very* enthusiastically.

About Saliva

Like it or not, saliva is a fact of life. And it usually seems as though there are only two salivary conditions: too much, and too little.

You have too little saliva if it is hard to keep your lips wet when sliding. If this is a problem, keep a glass of water handy.

You have too much saliva if it tends to get caught in the reeds of your harmonica to cause what I call **saliva blocks**. A saliva block temporarily causes the reed to get stuck, so that it doesn't seem to want to play. Fortunately, inhaling or exhaling with vigor will always remove a saliva block.

If saliva blockage becomes a problem for you, to play with your head tilted slightly up, so that any excess saliva tends to stay in your mouth. (I know that it sounds yucky, but after all, it *was* there in the first place, wasn't it?)

Salivation can actually be consciously controlled, but it takes years of practice. If you don't believe that, think of a lemon. A juicy, yellow, lemon, cut with a knife, just oozing with lemon juice. Did your thought of a lemon cause a salivary response? If so, you're on your way to mastery of the unappreciated art of salivary control!

More Exciting Blues: The Draw Jamm Blues In D!

Although the Bouncy Blowin' Jamm based on the C Major Scale certainly doesn't sound wrong, it doesn't sound all that bluesy, either. You'll find that the following licks and jamms, roughly based on the D Blues Scale (much more on that, later) sound more exciting. In fact, even though this style of playing uses only the In notes, we can approximate some of the licks of the late, great, master harmonicist, **Marion "Little Walter" Jacobs**.

Why It Works

This Draw Jamm Blues style of playing, using only In notes, works because almost all of the available In notes (without using the slide button) are notes that form the D minor chord. You can read a little more about chords on page 105, or you can just play for now, and worry about why it works later, because what you most need to know about this style of playing is that it does work. Try it yourself!

Simply play any combination of In notes along with either my D minor chord backing on the cassette, or with a friend who can play a D minor chord on guitar or keyboard. It works! If you can't think of anything to play on your own, read the next section, and try some of the suggested licks. This is one of the easiest, but most satisfying, things to do with your chromatic harmonica! See the Accompaniment Appendix if you don't have a friendly local guitar or keyboard player.

In Articulation

We generally think of inarticulate people as those who cannot express themselves very well. Yet on the harmonica, the ability to in-articulate allows us to express ourselves very well indeed!

It's easy to do harmonica articulation on the exhale — as easy as talking, which most of us practice for hours each day. It's not quite as easy to articulate on the In breath. In fact, it may take as much as a few moments of practice to get the hang of it! So give it a try, but please don't feel discouraged or be hard on yourself if it doesn't come naturally or instantly. It's not a natural thing to do. So begin working on In articulations, but don't get hung up here.

Remember thinking about the "Da" and "Ka" tongue motions involved in articulation? Say a few "Da's" right now, focusing your attention on your tongue. Empty your lungs, shut your nose, and see if you can say a few "Da's" on the inhale. Begin with your tongue pushed up against the roof of your mouth, and try to inhale (but your tongue is blocking all air from entering). Suddenly, let your tongue fall, and a "Da" will shoot in! For In articulations, **"Doo"s** or **"Too"s** may feel more natural than "Da"s.

See if you can whisper a few inhaled "Da"s or "Doo"s, without your harp. Remember, start with lungs **empty,** mouth close to single hole width, or at least not too wide, and nose **shut**, so that no air escapes through it. As it starts to feel a bit more natural after a moment of practice, try that familiar old "Dirty Dirty Dog", or "Doo Doo DooDoo Doo"...on the inhale!

Practice some In articulations through the 45 chord. If "Dirty Dirty Dog" is hard to inhale, try "Doodoo Doodoo Doo", or "Tootoo Tootoo Too". You may find that when articulating on an In note, it's easier if your lips are as close to a single note opening as you can manage (or at least no more than two holes wide).

All of the Dirty Dog articulation patterns, and the licks for *Out* notes on pages 24-31 can be played now as In licks. Use the same articulation patterns and/or hole numbers, but breathe In instead of Out. Here's an example — but please don't limit yourself to this one. Go back and use some of the others too!

•	•	•	•		•	•	•	•
Dirty	**Dirty**	**Dog**			**Dada**	**Dada**	**Da**	
56	56	67			56	56	67	
In	In	In			In	In	In	

	•	•	•	•	•	• • •
	Dirty	**Dirty**	**Ding**	**Dong**	**Dog**	
	56	56	67	67	56	
	In	In	In	In	In	

Glidin' In Rhythms

Of course, not all In licks require articulation — some licks glide smoothly from note to note. It's just as easy to glide while breathing in as it is to glide on the out breath, so try some gliding In licks, like the following. Remember to keep your lips wet for these!

This next one slides from 8 to 1, then back to 6, all on the In notes. If the timing seems difficult to understand, just concentrate on hitting the 8 on the first beat, the 1 on the second, and the 6 on the third. If you do that while keeping your lips on the harp and breathing in continuously, the in-between notes will take care of themselves. If you have trouble ending up on 6, keep a fingertip on top of the harp just above that hole, and aim the middle of your lips for it. And don't worry too much — this lick will sound fine if you use slightly different In notes than mine — try some!

```
•              •              •      •
8 7 6 5 4 3 2 1 2 3 4 5 6
I I I I I I I I I I I I I
```

For an exciting 16 beat gliding lick, play the above four beat lick twice, and then this eight beat version once.

```
•                    •              • • •    • • •
8 7 6 5 4 3 2 1 2 3 4 5 6 6 5
I I I I I I I I I I I I I I I
```

Jumpin' In Licks

We did it on the Out notes, and we'll do it on the Ins! Practice jumping from 1 to 5, then try this sixteen beat jumpin' lick, with a glide at the end. And make up some jump In licks of your own, using any combination of In notes.

```
•  •  •  •  •  •  •  •  •  •  •  •  •  •  •  •
1  5  1     1  5  1     1  5  1  5  1     54321
I  I  I     I  I  I     I  I  I  I  I     I  I
```

About the Warble

The tone effect that most harp players call a **warble** is created by alternating very rapidly between two holes that are next to each other, like 5 and 6 In, or 2 and 3 In (which are probably the most common warble combinations for chro). In my notation, I'll indicate a warble by putting a line like this ≈≈≈ under the notes that I want you to warble.

You can get a warble by keeping your mouth in good single note position while moving the harmonica rapidly back and forth so that your mouth covers each note for a tiny fraction of a second. This requires both good single noting skills and good hand/harp co-ordination, but it's a nice effect, so work at it.

The warble can be used almost anywhere. Try adding an eight beat warble pattern (with two beats of silence, for your breathing pleasure) to any of the In licks above. Play one of the licks (perhaps the sixteen beat glide pattern), then the eight beat warble (once or twice, for sixteen beats, as you prefer), then repeat the sixteen beat glide pattern, or a slight variation of it.

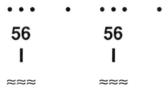

Notice Little Walter's use of the warble in the song discussed in the next section. It occurs approximately one minute into the song, and is probably on the 9 and 10 In notes. If you have an eight hole chromatic, you can play it on the 5 and 6 In.

In the Style of the Immortal *Little Walter*

Although he was indisputably one of the finest harmonica players ever to live and die in the blues, we can easily play in Little Walter's style using our In licks in the key of D on chromatic. The following licks are similar to some that Walter used in his classic chromatic song ***Teenage Beat***.

This song is perhaps his best example of chromatic work. It has a frantic, hyperactive quality, as befits its title.

It is widely available (along with all other Little Walter songs discussed in this book) on the Chess Blues Master Series Little Walter album (Chess 2 ACMB-202). Any good record store should be able to find you a new or used copy of this album — it's a no excuses, must-have item for every harpist.

Walter is playing a sixteen hole chromatic, most likely a Hohner 64. Hear how he uses the entire harp, from low to high end. As I mentioned earlier, the 1 - 4 holes on the sixteen hole models are one octave lower than the 1 - 4 holes on the eight or twelve holers. Listen to his work in *Teenage Beat* with the gutsy low end, at about 45 seconds, and at about one minute and 20 seconds into the song. Walter's beautiful throat vibrato, his subtle bending (these advanced techniques are considered below), and his heavy but careful use of microphone and amplifier distortion make everything he does sound great. Note: Walter uses a great deal of **octave blocking** (page 46).

Teenage Beat is in the key of D, so you can easily play along with it with your chromatic. Here are two versions of an eight beat lick located approximately one minute and 25 seconds into this two minute and 58 second song. Play them each a few times now, or jamm along with Walter or with me if you've got the record or my tape. We'll make these licks into an entire blues song, later on. If the rhythm seems tricky, you might want to think of each eight beat portion of the lick as a dirty dog rhythm, as follows.

•	•	•	•		•		•		•	•
dog	dog	dog			da	dir	ty	dir	ty	dog

•	•	•	•		•		•		•	•
56	56	56			4	5	6	5	4	5
I	I	I			I	I	I	I	I	I
≈≈≈	≈≈≈	≈≈≈								

•	•	•	•		•		•		•	•
4	4	4			3	4	5	4	3	4
I	I	I			I	I	I	I	I	I

The first line of the following sequence is similar to another *Teenage Beat* theme, one that occurs about one minute and 50 seconds into the song. The second line is a variation that I created to make the theme sound "finished" when played by itself. Notice that there are two whole beats of 5 In, then one half beat of 5 In and one half beat of 4 In (they share the same beat) then one entire beat of silence before the beat of 6 In. Check out the dog rhythm, if you need to, before playing the licks.

•		•		•		•		•		•	•	•
dog		dog		dirty				dog				

```
 •    •    •         •    •  •••          •    •    •         •    •  •••
 5    5    5    4         6              5    5    5    4         3
 I    I    I    I         I              I    I    I    I         I

 •    •    •         •    •  •••          •    •    •         •    •  •••
 5    5    5    4         6              7    6    5    4         1
 I    I    I    I         I              I    I    I    I         I
```

A Brief Walter Chromatic Discography

I'll use more examples and illustrations from Little Walter's work as I introduce new effects and ways of playing. If you have any of his work, and especially his chromatic songs *Teenage Beat*, *Thunderbird*, *Flying Saucer*, and *Blue Lights*, now is the time to start listening.

Once again, the Chess double album (Chess 2 ACMB-202) contains all of these songs, and many, many more that do not utilize chromatic. In fact, of the four songs mentioned, only *Teenage Beat* uses chromatic throughout the song. In *Thunderbird*, the first three verses use the standard ten hole non-chromatic harmonica (Key of G harp played in "second position"), and the last five feature chromatic. In *Flying Saucer*, the introduction and first two verses only are chromatic. In *Blue Lights*, the first verse and I believe the last verse are chromatic, but he applies so much distortion from his microphone and amplifier that it's hard to tell about the last verse (part of it may be non-chromatic).

Creating Your Own In Licks (and a 40's sound)

Almost any combination of In notes will sound reasonably good, if played with rhythm and feeling. Here's a moody little piece that I picked up from a 40's detective movie starring Humphrey Bogart as, I believe, Raymond Chandler's Philip Marlowe. It's in the key of D.

Play it a few times without stopping, and swing the beat: that is, hold the notes under the dots (the downbeats) longer than the notes that don't fall under dots. If you can bend notes at all (see page 47), bend the 6 each time it comes up, for a delightfully slinky, insinuating, 40's gun moll sound. Make up some similar combinations of your own, using mainly (but not exclusively) the In notes from 4 to 6, and featuring the 5 In or 1 In (D notes) prominently.

```
 •       •   •   •   •      •   •   •   •
 4   5   6   5      4   5   6   5
 I   I   I   I      I   I   I   I


 •       •   •      •   •      •   •      •   •      • ••••••
 4   5   6   5   4   5   4   3   4   3   2   3   2   1   5
 I   I   I   I   I   I   I   I   I   I   I   I   I   I   I
```

A Draw Jamm Blues Session

Can you put together what you've learned so far? Articulated In licks and glides, jumps and single note patterns a' la Walter...It may be easier to do with my background music (in the Key of D), but even if you're playing solo — turn the lights down low, relax your mind, put chro to mouth and let it flow!

The In and Out Jamm Blues In D

Have you really begun to master the ins and outs of harping? Can you tell an inhale from an exhale? Now's the time to find out — the time to gain full conscious control of what has been natural (and necessary) since birth — your breath!

By learning to integrate some Out notes into the In licks and patterns that you're already playing, you'll be able to play lots of blues in the style of Little Walter. By the way, I don't mean to imply that Little Walter is the only chro player to use this style. Other fine harmonicists, like the late **George "Harmonica" Smith**, and his living protegés **Rod Piazza** and **William Clarke**, often play similarly, using the chromatic largely in the Key of D, without too much (if any) slide button usage.

Why It Works

When we play this new style of music, we'll use both In and Out notes, while emphasizing the Ins. And when you study the D Blues Scale (on page 76), you'll see that of the seven available notes (D, F, A, and B on the In breath, and C, E, and G on the Out), five are used to form the D Blues Scale. That's why the In and Out Jamm Blues in D work. Now play some!

A Bluesy Breathing Pattern

By learning to breath in a particular pattern, you'll be able to form bluesy sounding licks anywhere on the chromatic harmonica. Try breathing as notated below. You may want to practice the breathing pattern without the harp, at first. Make your changes from In to Out breath quick and forceful. Swing the beat by holding the Ins just a tiny bit longer than the Outs, and hitting them just a bit harder.

•		•		•		•
dir	ty	dir	ty	dog		
In	Out	In	Out	In		

Now practice the pattern through the harp, on holes 5 and 6. It works better on chords than on single notes.

•		•		•		•
56	56	56	56	56		
In	Out	In	Out	In		

If that feels okay, try it on any two holes, like the 1 and 2 holes, or on the 4 and 5, or on the 6 and 7.

Movin' It Around

Perhaps the greatest beauty of this In/Out pattern style of playing is that once we learn the pattern, we can apply it anywhere. Simply move around while you maintain the In - Out - In - Out - In pattern of breath. Here are two four beat examples, one going down, the other up.

•		•		•		•		•		•		•
67	67	56	56	34		12	23	23	45	45		
I	O	I	O	I		I	O	I	O	I		

You can use the breath pattern while gliding, also. In this four beat lick, the glide from 1 to 8 occurs on the first In breath, just before the first actual beat of the lick. This is called *anticipating* the beat.

	•		•		•		•
da	dir	ty	dir	ty	dog		

	•		•		•		•
12345678	<u>78</u>	<u>67</u>	<u>56</u>	<u>56</u>	<u>12</u>		
	In	Out	In	Out	In		

Two Eight Beat Versions

Try this eight beat breathing pattern, which can be used in the same way as the four beat one, with any notes, jumping and gliding.

•		•		•	•	• • •
dir	ty	dir	ty	ding	dong	dog
In	Out	In	Out	In	Out	In

Practice it without the chro for a while, then use it on the 5 and 6 holes for a moment. Then, it's time to take your new eight beat breathing pattern on the road, and move it all around the harp, like this:

•		•		•	•	• • •
<u>67</u>	<u>67</u>	<u>56</u>	<u>56</u>	<u>23</u>	<u>23</u>	1
In	Out	In	Out	In	Out	In

And here's one last eight beat breathing pattern, with example. But I don't really want to tell you which notes to use. I want you to make up licks of your own, using any of these breathing patterns. What sounds good to you?

•		•		•		•		•		•		•	•
dir	ty	dir	ty	dir	ty	dir	ty	dir	ty	dir	ty	dog	
I	O	I	O	I	O	I	O	I	O	I	O	I	

•		•		•		•		•		•		•	•
<u>78</u>	<u>78</u>	<u>67</u>	<u>67</u>	<u>56</u>	<u>56</u>	<u>45</u>	<u>45</u>	<u>34</u>	<u>34</u>	<u>23</u>	<u>23</u>	<u>12</u>	
I	O	I	O	I	O	I	O	I	O	I	O	I	

The Sixteen Beat In and Out Lick

And, of course, we can create a sixteen beat breathing pattern by combining two of the four beat breathing patterns and one of the eight beat breathing patterns. Here's an example of that (one of my favorites):

•	•	•	•		•	•	•	•	•
<u>67</u>	<u>67</u>	<u>56</u>	<u>56</u>	<u>34</u>		<u>67</u>	<u>67</u>	<u>56</u>	<u>56</u>	<u>34</u>
I	O	I	O	I		I	O	I	O	I

•		•		•		•		• • •
<u>67</u>	<u>67</u>		<u>56</u>	<u>56</u>		<u>23</u>		<u>23</u>	1
I	O		I	O		I		O	I

Some Good Walter Style In and Out Licks

Walter, being a master harpist, did not have to rely on the simplified In and Out method of creating licks. In fact, since I (to the best of my knowledge) invented that method in the past decade, it could have had but scant influence on his playing. But once you get used to integrating both In and Out notes into your playing, you can easily play licks similar to some of his. And some of his licks can be approximated by the In/Out method.

Especially good examples of these in *Teenage Beat* occur in the song around seconds :56, 1:02, 1:12, and between 1:38 and 1:48. And just after the guitar solo ends at 2:27, he plays something similar to one of my favorite In and Out licks. He may be bending 2 In down to provide the note that I've written here as 2 Out. He then plays it a second time, with some added flourishes.

• • • • • •		•	•	•		• • • • • • •
3		3	3	2	2		1
I		O	I	I	O		I

Illustrating the use of just a hint of Out in a mostly In lick is this one, similar to the lick with which he starts *Teenage Beat*. Walter puts a bending effect on many of the notes when he plays his, and I've simplified the timing. Listen to the real thing, on this and on all of his chro work!

•	• • • • • ••		•	•	•	• •	•	•	• • • • • ••
5	6		5	6	5	4	3	2	1
I	I		I	I	I	O	I	I	I

And he ends the song with a whole series of sweet, poignant little licks, similar to this variation. The last three notes are one quick glide.

•	•		•		•	•	•		•	•	•
6	6	6	5	4	3	6	6	6	5	4	3
I	I	O	I	I	I	I	I	O	I	I	I

The In and Out Jamm Session

You now have lots of ways to create licks that will sound great, together or separately. Try playing *any* combination of your D based licks, that is, the Draw Jamm or In and Out Jamm styles. If you have the tape that accompanies this book, listen to how I combine many of the D licks that I've presented into one long jamm.

If you don't have my cassette but do have the Chess Little Walter double album to play along with, play try jamming with the four songs mentioned. Or read the Accompaniment Appendix, and round up a friendly musician, or even record some backing yourself as I describe!

The I'm a Person Type Lick in D

Here is one of my favorite In and Out licks, similar to the one used by Muddy Waters (and many other blues players) in his unforgettable *I'm A Man* and *Mannish Boy* songs. It is a four beat lick with two beats of silence during which you can insert either two beats of In licks or In/Out licks. It sounds great, and allows you freedom to improvise while maintaining a very consistent sound due to the repeated lick. This lick has a *three* beat countoff.

da	**dir**	**ty**	**dog**		**da**	**dir**	**ty**	**dog**	
	•		•	• •		•		•	• •
1	3	2	1	(insert licks)	1	3	2	1	(insert licks)
I	O	I	I		I	O	I	I	

Here are four examples of licks (in lighter type) that you might insert into the two beats of silence. Make up some of your own, too!

da	dir	ty	dog						da	dir	ty	dog				
•	•	•	•	•	•	•	•		•	•	•	•	•	•	•	•
1	3	2	1	1	1	1	1		1	3	2	1	3	3	2	2	1
I	O	I	I	I	I	O	I		I	O	I	I	I	O	I	O	I

da	dir	ty	dog						da	dir	ty	dog				
•	•	•	•	•	•	•	•		•	•	•	•	•	•	•	•
1	3	2	1	5	5	4	5		1	3	2	1	6	6	5	5	5
I	O	I	I	I	I	I	I		I	O	I	I	I	O	I	O	I

Dave's Faves: The Pseudo D Blues Scale

One of my favorite things to do in this style is to play a simplified version of the D Blues Scale. Although this scale should actually require use of the slide button, this easy version doesn't sound half bad, and noodling around with it for a few minutes (or hours, or days, or years — there's lots of meat on this one) will help prepare you for when we attempt the real thing. Remember that 4 and 5 Out (and 8 Out and 9 Out) are the same note. So use either one, but make sure you know which one you are on, since 4 In and 5 In (and 8 In and 9 In) are very different. In the actual version of the D Blues Scale (page 76), the first of the two 3 In notes would really be a 3 Out with the slide button pushed, and the first of the two 7 In notes would be a 7 Out with the slide button pushed. But wait until a bit later to try that!

1	2	3	3	3	4	5		5	6	7	7	7	8	9
I	I	O	I	I	O	I		I	I	O	I	I	O	I

Play that some, both left to right and right to left. Then, try making any combinations of these notes...they've got to sound bluesy. Here's a little something I like to fool around with. Can you work out some variations to it?

•	•	•	•	•	•	•	•
5	5	4	3	5	5	4	3	3	2	1	2
I	I	O	I	I	I	O	I	O	I	I	I

```
 •  •        •       •    •    •    •    •
 3  3  3  2  1  1  1
 I  O  I  I  I  O  I


 •     •       •    •    •    •    •    •
 1  1  2  2  3  3  4  5  6
 I  I  I  I  O  I  O  I  I


 •     •       •       •    •    •    •    •
 7  7  7  7  7  7  6  5
 I  O  I  O  I  O  I  I
```

Try adding some Out notes to the 40's Sound on page 38: Experiment!

```
 •     •    •    •    •       •    •    •
 4  5  6  5     4  5  6  5
 I  I  I  I     I  I  I  I


 •     •    •       •    •       •    •    •
 4  5  6  6  6  7  6  5  5
 I  I  I  O  I  O  I  I  I
```

What to Do Next

Now that you have the basic chromatic technique under some degree of control, it's time to study enough music theory (don't worry, not too much) so that you can understand and play blues and jazz chord structures. It's also time to learn about some advanced chromatic techniques.

Please notice that I said "time to learn about" these advanced techniques, not "time to learn them". If you want to keep up your playing momentum, don't spend too much time on the following advanced techniques, because they will take a long time to master, and you can and should always come back to work on them some more. Just knowing that they exist, and experimenting with them occasionally, is enough for now.

Three Advanced Techniques

I can already hear some of you saying "but I'm not an advanced player". I'll buy that, but I hope that someday you will be, and these techniques will then be important to you. So you might as well begin experimenting with them now. Besides, they can be used to make what you are already doing sound better, and thus well worth working on even for advanced beginners. These effects will all be easier to learn if you listen lots, both to my recorded examples, and to professional chro players.

Forked Tongue Blocking (Octave Blocking)

This type of tongue blocking is the technique of covering four (or very rarely five) holes with your mouth, as though you were playing an extremely large chord, and then blocking off the middle two holes with the tip of your tongue. It is often called octave blocking, since it can be used to play octave notes (the two C notes of 1 and 4 out, for instance, or the two D notes of 1 and 5 in). However, it also can be used to play non-octave notes, like the D and the B of 1 and 4 in). It's a must for D blues!

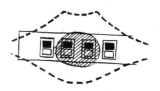 

Your tongue, soft and squishy as it is, will have to be pushed into the harmonica hard enough to flatten it enough to cover two holes (the three holes covered tongue position is much less often used). When using the two middle holes covered out of four holes tongue position, cover four with your mouth (say the 1, 2, 3, and 4), then use the tip of your tongue to locate the divider between holes 2 and 3. Center your tongue onto that divider, and press gently until your tongue flattens out somewhat. You will get a rich, full sound, somewhat more "tense" on the In than the Out.

Practice this on the 1 and 4 holes to start with. If you are not sure how to cover four holes at once, place a finger over the 5 hole. When your tongue is properly centered, you will be able to hear the 1 and the 4 hole sound at once.

When this tongue position becomes familiar on the <u>14</u> In and Out chords, focus your attention on the 1 hole as you play the <u>14</u>. Feel how an opening is created between the left side of your mouth and the left side of your tongue, and between the right side of your mouth and the right side of your tongue. Play a <u>14</u> chord, then remove your mouth from the harp without changing your mouth and tongue at all. Replace it on the <u>14</u> holes, and make sure that your tongue still covers the 2 and 3 holes.

When you can do the above reliably, move that left hand opening so that it covers the 2 hole instead of the 1, while taking care not to alter the position of your tongue and mouth in any other way. You will then be covering the holes 2, 3, 4, and 5 with your mouth, and

3 and 4 with your tongue. Before too long, you'll be able to play lots of licks and riffs using this technique, especially when playing Draw Blues in D.

Most of the licks that I've given you can be tongued like this. Just get your mouth into four hole tongue block position, and locate the original note (which will become the leftmost of four) with the left hand opening of your tongue blocked mouth.

The Throat Vibrato

We can give any note a lovely wavering tone with the throat vibrato. Although it is more effective on In notes than Out notes, it is easiest to learn on the Out breath. See if you can cough *very* gently, as though you were whispering the cough. Then begin practicing a controlled series of whispered coughs, rather as if you were making machine gun noises at a friend, but in the library. Do this on a variety of Out notes, and when it feels like each tiny cough comes smoothly, do it on the In notes. Most people require four to six months of practice before they can produce a decent throat vibrato at will.

On Bending

Since I've already written an entire book on the subject (see page 111), I'll just describe bending briefly here. It involves obtaining a single note, and then raising your tongue slightly in your mouth to partially block the airway. This, if done properly, will cause the note to dip down. For some people, saying "oy-you" approximates the necessary tongue movement, with "oy" approximating the unbent tongue position, and "you" the bent position.

Here's the easiest way to begin bending. Start by obtaining a clear single note, not too loud (5, 6, and 7 In are good ones to start on). While continuing to play the note, gently hump the middle of your tongue up towards the roof of your mouth, while increasing your volume slightly. This should cause the note to sound a bit lower. Block the airway too much (by raising your tongue up too high), and all sound will disappear. Experiment, and listen to my recorded examples.

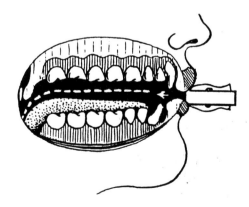 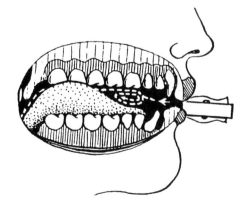

Practice holding a note, and bending and unbending it smoothly and repeatedly, with the mouth motion "oy-you oy-you oy-you oy-you oy-you".

When bending Out notes, you may find that going from an "ahh" mouth position to a "hiss" mouth position will approximate the motion needed.

Once you've learned to begin a note normally, and then bend it down, start trying to *begin* a note with a slight bend, then let it return to normal. Do this by starting to play the note with your mouth in bend position, then relax your tongue — and the note will unbend.

Stevie Wonder and Toots Thielemans often use this technique on their licks. I think of this as a "doo-wah", since I begin the note with a "doo" (with the middle of my tongue raised into bend position, but with its tip touching my upper front teeth), then relax it into normal "ah" position, laying flat and tensionless. Done quickly, it sounds like a "dwah", and can be used to accent almost any note or series of notes. The trick is to realize that we can move the tip and the middle or back of our tongues *independently*.

A "cheating" method of obtaining a bend is to tilt the front of your chro up while getting a clear single note. This will position your lower lip so that it partially blocks the hole. Although it may give you a bent sound (if you don't block the hole completely, and get no sound at all), it is hard to control your bending this way, so try to use the tongue method...

Chord Structures and the Blues

As I said earlier, harmonicists often like to play along with chords played by other musicians (whom we can call accompanists), like guitarists, pianists, or other combinations of instrumentalists. Rather than playing just one single chord, however, the accompanists usually play a repeated sequence of two or more chords. This is called a **chord structure**.

When we are playing lead harmonica along with accompanists who are providing the chord structure, we can consider the chord structure as a skeleton which we will flesh out by our playing. At other times, either because we are playing solo or because we are providing chord structure accompaniment for other musicians, we must be able to play the notes of the proper chords at the proper times.

An Easy Chord Structure to Jamm With

One of the easiest chord structures to jamm along with on chro is the chord structure that is made of a D minor and a C Major chord. Each verse of this structure consists of eight beats of D minor followed by eight beats of C Major. This chord structure is often found in Reggae music, and sometimes in R & B.

We can play along with this structure simply by playing any In note during the D minor chord, and any Out note during the C Major chord.

••••••••　　　　　••••••••

D minor　　　　**C Major**　　　　　**(then repeat)**

Any In Note Jamm　　**Any Out Note Jamm**

But a far more common chord structure, indeed *the* most common, is the Twelve Bar Blues Structure, below.

The Twelve Bar Blues Structure

There is one type of chord structure that is more widely used than any other: the Twelve Bar Blues Structure. As you doubtless recall, a bar is a musical term that usually (for our types of music) refers to four beats.

A twelve bar blues structure (often called just a Twelve Bar or a Blues Structure) is made up of three chords that are stacked together in a particular order to form each verse. These chords have a very specific relationship to each other, so that once we choose the first chord of a twelve bar, we know what the other two must be.

There are two ways of referring to the chords of a blues structure. We can use the letter names of the chords, and speak of a blues in the Key of C that uses the chords C Major, F Major, and G7. Similarly, a blues in the Key of D uses the chords D Major, G Major, and A7. Or we can use the *generic* roman numeral terms and refer to the **I chord**, the **IV chord**, and the **V** or **V7 chord**. Lots of musicians use these numerical terms (pronounced "one", "four", and "five" chord), so it's important to know this way of referring to the chords of a blues structure.

A 12 bar blues structure is constructed as follows:

I chord for 16 beats or 4 bars	In a C Blues, for instance, a C chord
IV chord for 8 beats or 2 bars	In a C Blues, this is an F chord
I chord again for 8 beats or 2 bars	The C chord, again
V7 chord for 4 beats or 1 bar	In a C Blues, this is a G7 chord
IV chord again for 4 beats or 1 bar	The F chord, again
I chord for 8 beats or 2 bars	The C chord, once again

Now do it all over again without a pause, for another verse!

Blues and jazz musicians often use a musical device known as a **turnaround,** which is a few beats of V7 chord thrown in during the end of the last I chord. This lets everybody listening know that one verse is ending, and another verse is about to begin.

If you have my tape, listen to me play some twelve bars while you look at the chart above. If you don't, why not play a few twelve bars of your own right now? I'll present both a Twelve Bar Blues in the Key of C, and a Twelve Bar Blues in the Key of D. These are the two easiest keys for chromatic players to begin with, and each allows us to create very different types of music, as I'll demonstrate later on.

It's really important to familiarize yourself with the structure of a twelve bar blues. Study the chart above, and learn the names of the chords, when the chords change, and how long each chord lasts for. This will help when you are looking at the notation for many of the blues solos later on in the book.

The Simplest Twelve Bar Blues in C

It's possible to play a very simplified but accurate twelve bar using only one note each for the I chord, the IV chord, and the V7 chord. Here's a **Blues Structure in C**. Because we are going to play a Blues in C, by definition we will begin it with a C chord, that is, our I chord will be a C Major chord. We'll be using 1 Out to represent the C chord.

Our IV chord will be an F Major chord, and we'll use a 2 In note to represent the F chord. Our V7 chord will be a G7 chord, and we'll use a 3 Out note to represent the G7 chord. Play each note three times, for one beat each, then use one beat of silence to breathe and rest in. Feel free to use some articulation (perhaps a dirty dog pattern) for each bar. Ready?

C	C	C	C	F	F	C	C	G	F	C	C
••••	••••	••••	••••	••••	••••	••••	••••	••••	••••	••••	••••
1	1	1	1	2	2	1	1	3	2	1	1
O	O	O	O	I	I	O	O	O	I	I	I

On page 56, I'll present a Blues in C that uses all the notes of each chord, and sounds a lot more exciting. But practice this simple blues for now, so that you can hear exactly when each chord change takes place.

The Simplest Twelve Bar Blues in D

Now try a **Blues Structure in the Key of D**. In a D Blues, our I chord will be a D Major, our IV chord will be a G Major, and our V7 chord will be an A. We'll be using the D, G, and A notes to represent the D Major, G Major, and A7 chords. Articulate as you like, and don't forget to breathe. In this one I'll include a turnaround, which will be composed of a few beats of A note at the very end of the verse, followed by one beat of silence.

D	D	D	D	G	G	D	D	A	G	D	D	turn (A)
••••	••••	••••	••••	••••	••••	••••	••••	••••	••••	••••	••••	• • • •
1	1	1	1	3	3	1	1	3	3	1	1 3 3	
I	I	I	I	O	O	I	I	I	O	I	I I I	

Play the simple Blues in D until you don't even need to look at the above notation (very much). Then you'll be ready to play a more improvised blues, perhaps somewhat in the style of Little Walter, or maybe something a bit more structured, if you prefer.

A Walter Style Twelve Bar Blues

Although it is certainly possible to create great Blues in D by studying the D Blues Scale on page 76 and then, in true "head music" fashion, writing down and playing different combinations of blues scale notes, this is rarely done. Usually, D Blues are played from the gut, using the Draw Jamm and In and Out Jamm styles of playing, without much planning beforehand.

If you like, play along with some D Blues Backing (like the selection on my cassette, or find a guitarist or keyboard player friend to play some D Blues for you). As long as you are playing along with backing music, or with other musicians who can maintain the chord structure, you can simply play throughout the entire Twelve Bar using the Draw Jamm or In and Out Jamm methods. For instance, in the second full verse of *Flying Saucer* (from approximately second :27 to second :43 of the song, after the introduction and one verse) Little Walter repeats one 16 beat lick three times, with slight variations (the third time, he fades it out before we expect the turnaround to occur). Try playing something like this three times (with D Blues backing) for an exciting if unstructured Twelve Bar solo. It's based, theoretically speaking, on the Pseudo D Blues Scale, although of course Walter wasn't thinking about that when he blew it!

```
•••• ••••        •        •    •    •    •        •    •    •
 67             67   5    4    3    3    2    1
 I              O    I    I    I    O    I    I
 ≈≈≈
```

Twelve Bar Blues Jamms In D

If you'd prefer to create your own improvisation, you'll need to follow the structure a bit more closely. Do so by jamming as you please during the D parts of the verse, and use G notes during the G chords, and A notes during the A chords and turnaround, like this:

```
••••      ••••      ••••      ••••      ••••      ••••      ••••      ••••

any  In or In and Out licks                3         3        more   In/Out
                                           O         O
```

```
••••        ••••        •••• •              •    •    •
 3           3         more In/Out          3    3
 I           O                              I    I
```

You don't need to use *only* the 3 Out and 3 In notes during the G and A chords. If you like, you can emphasize some extra 3 Out notes during the G chord parts of the structure, and some 3 In notes during the A chord parts, but also use some other notes, like this:

```
••••    ••••    ••••    ••••      •   •      •   •   •   •      •    •
any  In  and  Out  licks          3   3   3  2   1   3   3   3  2
                                  O   I   O  I   I   O   I   O  I
```

```
••••    ••••    •   •      •   •          •   •       •   •
more In/Out      3   3   3   3            3   3   3   3   2
                 I   I   O   I            O   O   I   O   I
```

```
••••    •      •   •   •
more In/Out     5   3
                I   I
```

You'll be able to jamm more, and more satisfyingly, within a twelve bar structure when you have learned the D Blues Scale and C Blues Scale. Which you can go ahead and do right now, if you choose.

From Gut Music to Head Music

The Bouncy Blowing Jamms and the Draw Jamms that you were just playing are great examples of gut playing: not much to think about, and lots of feeling (I hope). So now might be a good time to work on some simple head playing, which means beginning to learn music theory, and beginning to practice chords and scales.

If you're not hung up on immediate gratification, these chords and scales will be essential when you eventually aspire to the jazzier Toots Thielemans or Stevie Wonder styles — so you might as well start workin' on them now. Or you can skip to the song sections on pages 60-65, or go on to the section on using the slide button (page 66), which will prepare you for playing the Blues Scales.

Just a Few More Notes About Music

The following section will only teach you a few musical terms, and give you a very general and oversimplified idea of why we play what we play. It is not meant to be a complete course in music theory. But it should give you enough information to let you play, plenty! Let's review for a moment, first...

• Playing any one harmonica hole at a time produces what we call a **note**.

• Playing any two or more holes that sound right together at the same time produces what we call a **chord**. Chords can be played on any instrument that can play more than one note at a time.

• There are three main types of chords. **Major chords** sound bright and bouncy. **Minor chords** sound plaintive or eerie. And **Seventh chords** sound somewhere in-between: a bit tense, or bluesy.

• Harmonica players often like to play along by improvising, or **"jamming"** with a chord or a set of chords played by another instrument, such as a guitar or keyboard.

Your First "Arpeggiated" Chords: C Major, F Major, and G7

Since you're working on single noting already anyway (I hope!), these **arpeggiated chords** shouldn't be too difficult. Arpeggiated just means that each note of the chord is played separately, rather than covering all of the holes with your mouth and playing them simultaneously. Of course, many chords, like the F or G7 below, can *only* be played in arpeggiated form, since some of the notes must be played on the In breath and others on the Out.

The C Major Chord

The simplest arpeggiated chord to play is the C Major chord, which is composed of a C note, an E note, and a G note. Here are a few different ways to play it.

1	2	3		5	6	7		9	10	11
O	O	O		O	O	O		O	O	O
C	E	G		C	E	G		C	E	G

The F Major Chord

Your next arpeggiated chord is the F Major chord, composed of an F note, an A note, and a C note. Here are a few different ways to play it.

2	3	4		6	7	8		10	11	12
I	I	O		I	I	O		I	I	O
F	A	C		F	A	C		F	A	C

The G Major Seventh Chord

Your last chord, for now, is the G Major Seventh chord, also known as G7 for short. It's a four note chord, made up of a G note, a B note, a D note, and an F note. Following are two ways to play it. Can you hear that the G7 sounds a bit more plaintive than the three note C and F Major chords? Soon you'll be using these three chords — C, F, and G7 — to play some exciting blues!

3	4	5	6		7	8	9	10
O	I	I	I		O	I	I	I
G	B	D	F		G	B	D	F

Your Arpeggio Blues, In C

Here is a Twelve Bar Blues based on the three chords you've just been practicing. Drop the last note of the G7 chord for now, and it's easy! Use an entire G chord in the last bar (which could also be a bar of C, if you chose not to use a turnaround) for a turnaround. Flow smoothly from one note to another, or start each one with a sharp dah sound — whatever sounds best to you.

```
  •    •    •         •    •    •         •    •    •         •    •    •    •
  1    2    3         1    2    3         1    2    3         1    2    3
  O    O    O         O    O    O         O    O    O         O    O    O
  C    E    G         C    E    G         C    E    G         C    E    G


  •    •    •         •    •    •         •    •    •         •    •    •    •
  2    3    4         6    7    8         1    2    3         1    2    3
  I    I    O         I    I    O         O    O    O         O    O    O
  F    A    C         F    A    C         C    E    G         C    E    G


  •    •    •         •    •    •         •    •    •         •    •    •    •
  3    4    5         2    3    4         1    2    3         3    4    5
  O    I    I         I    I    O         O    O    O         O    I    I
  G    B    D         F    A    C         C    E    G         G    B    D
```

Now try the same thing, but break the first note of each of the chords into two parts with a dada type articulation, for some rhythmic excitement. Here is what the first two bars of the above verse would look like, played that way. Try doing this for each bar of *each* chord.

```
  •         •         •         •         •         •         •         •
  1    1    2         3         1    1    2         3
  O    O    O         O         O    O    O         O
```

Or break the second note of each chord into two pieces, like this:

```
  •         •         •         •         •         •         •         •
  1         2    2    3         1         2    2    3
  O         O    O    O         O         O    O    O
```

Or break both notes into two pieces, and don't forget to swing!

```
  •         •         •         •         •         •         •         •
  1    1    2    2    3         1    1    2    2    3
  O    O    O    O    O         O    O    O    O    O
```

The Inversion Blues

We don't always have to play the notes of a chord in their "normal" order. In fact, sometimes they sound more interesting when played in *inverted*, or out-of-order, form. Here are some inversions of the lowest C chord.

2	3	1		2	3	4		3	1	2		1	3	2
O	O	O		O	O	O		O	O	O		O	O	O
E	G	C		E	G	C		G	C	E		C	G	E

Here's a Twelve Bar Blues in C based on a variety of inverted chords. After you've learned to play this one, see if you can experiment with re-arranging the notes of each chord to come up with some inverted twelve bars of your own.

	•		•	•	•
2	3	2	1		repeat three more times
O	O	O	O		

	•		•	•	•
3	4	3	2		repeat once more
I	O	I	I		

•		•	•	•		•		•	•	•
2	3	2	1			2	3	2	4	
O	O	O	O			O	O	O	O	

•		•	•	•		•		•	•	•
4	5	4	3			3	4	3	2	
I	I	I	O			I	O	I	I	

•		•	•	•		•		•	•	•
2	3	2	1			4	5	4	3	
O	O	O	O			I	I	I	O	

Scales, the "Alphabets" of Music

A scale is a specific group of notes, like the "Major Scale" (Do Re Mi Fa So La Ti Do) that you may already be familiar with. These specific notes provide the basic building blocks of a piece of music, just like the 26 letters of the alphabet provide the basic building blocks of any piece of writing. The letters of the Russian alphabet create Russian words, sentences, and long somber novels. Letters of the English alphabet create English words, sentences and literature. Scales are different musical alphabets. Three very different scales are most commonly used by harmonica players.

• The **Major Scale** has a bouncy, brassy sound. It is most often used for playing popular, classical, and American folk music.

• The **Minor Scale** has a more wistful or plaintive quality. It is often used in the music of the Gypsy people, in Eastern European music, and in Irish and Jewish folk music.

• The **Blues Scale** has, well, a bluesy feel. Some people consider it a compromise between the Major and Minor Scales, because it uses some notes from both. Developed by the Afro-American people, the Blues Scale is used today in blues, rock, soul, disco, funk and jazz music.

The sections just above and below this box will give you the minimum information that you need to know about scales. If you'd like to know more about music, please turn to Appendix A on page 99. You may at least want to look at the chart on Page 104 which compares these different scales. If you're really desperate to play a Blues Scale, turn to page 76 for a few minutes.

• The **Major Scale** is most often played in the Key of C. When playing the Key of C on a C harmonica, we begin our scale on the note C (there are three or four of them on your harp). It's easy to play folk, popular, and classical songs in C, because it's easy to play a Major Scale starting on C. But it's a bit harder to play blues in C, because it's harder to play a Blues Scale starting on C on a C chromatic, and takes lots of slide button work.

• The **Minor Scale** is most easily played in A on a C chromatic (this is called, obviously enough, "playing in A minor". When playing in A minor on a C harmonica, we begin our scale on the note A. It's easy to play haunting, beautiful, Minor songs in A minor, like *Greensleeves,* or *Summertime.* A variation of this scale, called the Dorian or Dorian Minor Scale, is most easily played in the key of D.

• The **Blues Scale** can be played most easily in the Key of D on a C chro. Playing the Blues Scale in D gives us blues music with a Minor, plaintive feel. When playing a Blues Scale in D on a C harmonica, we naturally begin our scale on the note D.

The C Major Scale

As I just said, C Major is a wonderfully easy and satisfying scale for playing folk and simple classical songs. After you've practiced this scale, you'll have no problems picking out the songs in the Key of C Major that follow.

If you can't get single notes yet, you can still begin playing the scales and songs below. But please continue to work on single noting, since it will become more and more necessary as you progress.

Now look carefully at the C Major Scale notation, then slowly begin to play it. Try to make sure that you end on the 4 Out note, and not the 5 Out note. They both sound exactly the same, but it is really important to know which hole you are on, especially when playing more complicated songs. Once the 1-4 hole C Major Scale feels comfortable to you, try the 5-8 hole C Major Scale (or other higher versions, if you have a twelve or sixteen holer) as well.

C	D	E	F	G	A	B	C
1	1	2	2	3	3	4	4
O	I	O	I	O	I	I	O

5	5	6	6	7	7	8	8
O	I	O	I	O	I	I	O

9	9	10	10	11	11	12	12
O	I	O	I	O	I	I	O

Also, it is helpful to be able to play the scale from its high end to its low end (that is, reading the notation from right to left), as well as from low to high. So go back, read the scale from the right to the left, and pick out the notes.

A Few Simple C Major Songs

The following are some songs to be played in the Key of C, that is, they are based on the C Major Scale. Of course, these same songs could be played in any key (using any Major Scale), but the C Major Scale is the easiest for beginners.

So — time to play! Choose the song that you know best, and try to play it while looking at the notation. There are really only two things to think about: which hole to use, and whether to inhale or exhale. Some of you will prefer to play just a few notes at a time, learning the song section by section. Others will want to plow through an entire song, mistakes and all. Do whatever feels best to you, but do it!

Oh When The Saints Go Marchin' In

	•		•••		•		•••
Oh	when	the	Saints	Go	mar	chin	in
1	2	2	3	1	2	2	3
O	O	I	O	O	O	I	O

	•		•	•	•	•	•••
Oh	when	the	Saints	Go	mar	chin	in
1	2	2	3	2	1	2	1
O	O	I	O	O	O	O	I

•		••		•	•		•		•	•
Yes	I	want	to	be	in	that	num	ber		
2	1	1	1	2	3	3	3	2		
O	I	O	O	O	O	O	O	I		

•		•	•	•	•	•••
When	the	saints	go	mar	chin	in
2	2	3	2	1	1	1
O	I	O	O	O	I	O

Frankie and Johnny

Fran	kie	an	John	ny	were	sweet	hearts
1	2	3	3	3	3	1	1
O	O	O	I	O	I	O	O

Lor	dy	but	how	they	did	love
1	2	3	3	3	2	1
O	O	O	I	O	O	O

They	were	in	true	love	to	geth	er
4	4	3	4	4	3	4	4
O	O	I	O	O	I	O	O

Like	the	stars	that	shine	a	bove
3	3	4	4	4	3	3
O	O	O	O	I	I	O

He	was	her	man
2	2	3	1
O	I	O	I

But	he	done	her	wrong	(but	he	done	her	wrong)
3	2	3	2	1	3	3	3	3	4
O	O	O	O	O	I	O	I	O	O

The A Minor Scale

As I said above, the poignant minor scale is the musical alphabet of ethnic music the world over. (Note: musicians usually capitalize the "M" of Major Scale, but leave the minor scale lower case. In standard chord notation, the word minor is abbreviated to the lower case letter m [as in Am], and the word Major to the upper case letter M [as in CM]).

If you've practiced the C Major Scale and songs, the A minor scale shouldn't seem difficult at all. Here are the places it can be played on the different size chromatic harmonicas.

Notice that the third note of the A minor scale can be played on either 4 Out or 5 Out. You can use whichever you like, *as long as you know* exactly where you are and are ready to locate the next note, 5 In, without hesitation.

After the 3-7 A minor scale feels familiar, practice playing it from the high end to the low end (that is, reading the notation from right to left). Then, if you have a larger harp, play the other A minor scale written below.

3	4	4 or 5	5	6	6	7	7
I	I	O	I	O	I	O	I

7	8	8 or 9	9	10	10	11	11
I	I	O	I	O	I	O	I

Greensleeves

I've changed two notes of this lovely traditional song so that you don't need to use the slide at all. Once you become friendly with the slide button as described in the next section, make this substitution: during the word "la-a-dy", which I've written 3 Out-2 Out-3 Out below, instead play 3 Out Slide-2 In Slide-3 Out Slide. It will sound even better!

·	··	·	·	·	·	··	·	·	·
A	las	my	lo	ve	you	do	me	wro	ng
3	4	5	6	6	6	5	4	3	3
I	O	I	O	I	O	I	I	O	I

·	··	·	·	·	·	··	·	··
to	cast	me	o	ut	dis	court	eous	ly
4	4	3	3	3	3	4	3	2
I	O	I	I	O*	I	I	O*	O

·	··	·	·	·	·	··	·	·	·
for	I	Do	love	you	with	all	my	hea	rt
3	4	5	6	6	6	5	4	3	3
I	O	I	O	I	O	I	I	O	I

·	·	·	·	·	·	·	···	··
and	who	but	my	la	a	dy	Green	sleeves
4	4	4	3	3	2	3	3	3
I	O	I	I	O	O	O	I	I

And here is the real McCoy — cheat down to the next section on slide button use, and give it a go if you like this lovely old song. And give the 3 Outs with asterisks a shot of slide button as well — you'll be glad you did.

·	·	·	·	·	·	·	···	··
and	who	but	my	la	a	dy	Green	sleeves
4	4	4	3	3	2	3	3	3
I	O	I	I	◎	◨	◎	I	I

If you know the song *Summertime* (it begins with the notes 6 Out - 5 Out - 6 Out when played in the key of A), try to pick it out.

The D Dorian Minor Scale

This tremendously useful scale can be used to play a number of great blues, jazz, and folk songs. It can be easily blended with the D Blues Scale, to which it is a close relation. And after you've learned the D Blues Scale, you can come back and improvise on these songs.

1	2	2	3	3	4	4 or 5	5
I	O	I	O	I	I	O	I

5	6	6	7	7	8	8 or 9	9
I	O	I	O	I	I	O	I

House of the Rising Sun

There	is	a	house	in	New	Or	leans
•		•		•		•	
3	5	5	4	3	3	2	1
I	I	I	O	I	O	I	I

That	they	call	the	Ris	ing	Sun
	•		•		•	
2	3	3	4	3	3	3
I	O	I	O	I	O	I

And	it's	been	the	ruin	of	ma	ny	poor	boys
	•		•		•			•	
3	4	5	5	4	3	3	3	2	1
I	O	I	I	O	I	O	O	I	I

Oh	me	I	kn	ow	I'm	one
	•		•		•	
2	1	2	2	2	2	1
I	I	I	O	I	O	I

St. James Infirmary

I couldn't resist including this terrific blues and jazz standard, even though it requires a single slide button note. If you know it and love it, you'll figure it out! And when you've mastered your D Blues Scale, you can come back to it and apply lots of slide button blues to all the 3 Out notes, the 6 Out, even to the 3 In (if you're sparing).

Feel free to throw some D jamms into the beats of silence. The 40's blues licks will work great in there, as will any D Blues Scale licks, or even any simple Walter style In only or In and Out jamms. Don't think to much about it — just listen to my increasingly jazzy verses on the tape, close your eyes, and feel for it! That's the blues!

Well	I	went	down	to	St.	James	In	firm	ry
1	2	3	3	2	3	3	3	2	1
I	I	I	I	I	O	I	O	I	I

My	ba	by	was	a	lay	in	there
1	3	3	3	3	6	5	3
I	I	I	I	I	O	I	I

All	laid	out	on	a	long	whi	ite	ta	ble
1	3	3	3	2	3	3	3	2	1
I	I	I	I	I	O	I	O	I	I

So	young	so	good	oh	lord	It	ain't	fair
1	2	1	2	3	3	3	2	1
I	I	I	I	O	◎	O	I	I

Try playing Summertime using this scale (it begins with the notes 7 In - 6 In - 7 In when played in the key of D).

Using the Chromatic Slide Button

Although most of the songs that we've been playing so far sound fine without the use of the slide button, now may be a good time to explore its use.

• From now on, I will indicate that the slide button is supposed to be pushed in by typesetting the letter I or O for that note in **outline** type. Following are a variety of exercises that will help you to become comfortable with the use of the slide button.

Play any single Out note, without using the slide. While holding the Out note, push the slide in, then release it. Notice that if you push the slide in very slowly, for a moment you hear both notes. Since the two notes that sound in this situation do not go together too well, you will always want to push the slide button all the way in (and release it all the way out) rapidly.

Now play any Out note, and push and release the slide button repeatedly, as quickly as you can. This produces an exciting sound that harp players usually call a **trill**.

To gain control over the slide, play this sequence, making sure that you play each note (the 1 Out and the 1 **Out** — that is, the 1 Out slide) for exactly one beat.

```
 •    •    •    •       •    •    •    •
 1    1    1            1    1    1         and repeat
 O    ◎    O            O    ◎    O
```

It's a bit trickier to use the slide while changing from an Out to an In note, or vice versa. You'll need to learn to push the slide button in just as you switch from the Out to the In. Try it, with these two exercises. In the first one, you'll switch from Out to In, *then* push the button. In the second one, you'll switch your breathing and push the button at the *same time*.

```
 •    •    •    •       •    •    •    •
 1    1    1            1    1    1         and repeat
 O    I    I            O    I    I
```

```
 •    •    •    •       •    •    •    •
 1    1    1            1    1    1         and repeat
 O    I    O            O    I    O
```

Also practice your **slide flutter**, which is what I call it when I move the slide in and out as quickly as possible. I indicate a flutter by outlining the number of *the hole number* on which to do the flutter *as well as* the I or O. So a three beat flutter on the 3 Out note (rapidly alternating the note 3 Out and the note 3 Out with slide pushed) would look like this, with a beat of silence to make it a four beat lick.

The Spoonful Style Lick

Interestingly enough, that next to the last exercise uses the same notes as a very famous blues/rock lick called the Spoonful lick. It comes from a great song (officially written by bluesman Willie Dixon and popularized by the rock group Cream, although probably derived from an older traditional blues) called, simply enough, *Spoonful.* Here's a lick similar to the main repeated lick of the song. It can be played on 1, 5, or 9. I prefer it on 5, myself. I'll write it out as an eight beat lick, since it's simpler to play that way at first, but it's actually a four beat lick, as written below.

```
 •      •      •      •     ••     •      •
 1      1      1      1      1      1
 ◊      O      ◊      O      ◊      O


 •      •      •      •     ••     •      •
 5      5      5      5      5      5
 ◊      O      ◊      O      ◊      O
```

And here it is as a four beat lick. Cut off the last note sharply, so that there is a bit of silence before you play it again:

```
 •             •             •      •
 1      1      1      1      1      1
 ◊      O      ◊      O      ◊      O
```

The I'm a Person Type Lick

If you've learned the simpler version of this great lick (on page 43), add one more note with your slide button, and sound even better!

	da	dir	ty	ol'	dog				da	dir	ty	ol'	dog			
		•		•		•	•			•		•		•	•	•
	1	3	3	2	1				1	3	3	2	1			
	I	◎	O	I	I				I	◎	O	I	I			

Insert any Draw note jamm, In and Out Jamm, 40's Style Jamm, or whatever seems to fit into the two beats of silence. Here are four examples of possible licks — make up lots more of your own.

	•			•		•		•		•		•	•		•
1	3	3	2	1	5	5	4	5	1	3	3	2	1	56	56	56
I	◎	O	I	I	I	I	I	I	I	◎	O	I	I	I	O	I

		•			•		•		•		•		•		•		•
1	3	3	2	1 4	4	5 6 5	1	3	3	2	1	3	3	3	3
I	◎	O	I	I I	I I I I I	I	◎	O	I	I	◎	O	◎	O

The Hoochie Coochie Person Type Lick

Since the timing on this classic style lick is the same as the one above that you just learned, I can't resist giving it to you, even though it doesn't require slide use. It, like the lick above, is in the key of D. And once again, try to fit some licks (note combinations that you've thought of ahead of time) or jamms (spontaneous improvisation that more or less fits) into the two beat silences.

	da	dir	ty	ol'	dog				da	dir	ty	ol'	dog			
		•		•		•	•			•		•		•	•	•
	3	5	3	5	5				3	5	3	5	5			
	I	O	I	O	I				I	O	I	O	I			

An Easy Slidin' Twelve Bar Blues

Here's an easy blues verse that will help you get used to moving the harp in your mouth while you work the slide button. It has a slightly eerie, almost minor feel, and no turnaround. Practice each line separately, then put 'em together. Make each note sing — clear and clean. This happens to be a blues in C. Note the trill flutters on the last note of each line.

```
•     •     •     •      •     •     •     •
1  1  1  2  2  3  3   1  1  1  2  ②
O  I  ◨  I  ◨  I  ◨   O  I  ◨  I  ◨


•     •     •     •      •     •     •     •
1  1  1  2  2  3  3   1  1  1  2  ②
O  I  ◨  I  ◨  I  ◨   O  I  ◨  I  ◨


•     •     •     •      •     •     •     •
2  3  3  4  4  5  5   2  3  3  4  ④
I  I  ◨  I  ◨  I  ◨   I  I  ◨  I  ◨


•     •     •     •      •     •     •     •
1  1  1  2  2  3  3   1  1  1  2  ②
O  I  ◨  I  ◨  I  ◨   O  I  ◨  I  ◨


•     •     •     •      •     •     •     •
3  4  4  5  5  6  6   2  3  3  4  ④
O  I  ◨  I  ◨  I  ◨   I  I  ◨  I  ◨


•     •     •     •      •     •     •     •
1  1  1  2  2  3  3   1  1  1  2  ②
O  I  ◨  I  ◨  I  ◨   O  I  ◨  I  ◨
```

A Tough Decision

It's time to make a choice, at least for a while. If you tend to be an eye or a head player, you probably liked the *Arpeggiated Blues in C* that you learned earlier, and you'll probably enjoy both the following chord work, and the more complex arpeggiated blues written out below.

But if improvisation, creating your own music, is more to your taste, you may prefer to skip down to the *Real Blues Scale In D*, and the C Blues Scale. After learning one or both of these scales, you can do some serious jamming.

It's your choice — both ways of making music sound great, to me. So please use the rest of this book in the way that seems rightest to you!

Some Slidin' C Seventh Chord Rhythms

Now that you can use the slide button, you can begin to play the more jazzy sounding seventh chords. Here are a few C7 chords. You may want to practice the 3 Out to 3 In slide for a moment before attempting the entire chord.

1	2	3	3		5	6	7	7		9	10	11	11
O	O	O	◖		O	O	O	◖		O	O	O	◖

Sound good, don't they? Once you can play them as written above, turn them into licks by adding a bit of rhythm, and an inversion or two. Try these three rhythm patterns on the low C7 chord, then apply the pattern to the middle one (or the high one, if you have a 12 holer). Then make up some rhythm patterns of your own, using the notes of the C7 chord. Hint: Playing the first of these three licks twice, then the last 8 beat lick once, creates a fine 16 beat lick!

•		•	•	•		••	•		•
1	2	3	3			3	3	2	1
O	O	O	◖			◖	O	O	O

•		•	•	•		•	•	•	•
1	2	3	3	3	2	1			
O	O	O	◖	O	O	O			

Slidin' the F Seventh Rhythms

While you're at it, might as well learn the F7 as well. Here are your F7's. They are a bit harder than the C7, because not only must you change from the Out breath to the In breath while moving the slide button in, you must also move up one hole. It's a lot to think about at one time, so practice the 4 Out to 5 In Slide (and the 8 - 9) separately until it feels comfortable, before moving on to the entire chord. And if you feel overwhelmed, go on to the G7 chord rhythms below — they don't even use the slide button!

```
4   5              8   9
O   ▯              O   ▯


            2   3   4   5       6   7   8   9
            I   I   O   ▯       I   I   O   ▯
```

If the F7's don't seem terribly hard, throw some rhythm onto them. The second rhythm pattern is nearly as hard as anything in this book, so don't be discouraged if you have trouble with it. Just go on to the G7 rhythms, or to the easier blues jamms in the next section...

```
 •       •   •   •          •       •   •       •
 2   3   4   5              2   3   4   5   4   3
 I   I   O   ▯              I   I   O   ▯   O   I
```

The Easy G7 and G#7 Chord Rhythms

Now for an easy 16 beat G7 rhythms. It sounds great, but doesn't even have a drop of slide work to worry about. Practice the lines separately, them put 'em together!

```
 •       •   •   •          •       •   •       •
 3   4   5   6              3   4   5   6   5   4
 O   I   I   I              O   I   I   I   I   I


 •       •   •   •       •   •   •   •
 3   4   5   6   5   4   3
 O   I   I   I   I   I   O
```

And while we're at it, the G#7 (pronounced G sharp seven) chord looks scary, but it's really very easy. Simply play a G7 chord with the slide button in, and presto, a G#7 chord! Then play alternating G#7 and G7 chords. Add a bit of rhythm, and you've got a great, jazzy, sound! Try it.

3	4	5	6
◎	◖	◖	◖

•		•	•	•		•		•	•	•	
3	4	5	6			3	4	5	6		**Play repeatedly**
◎	◖	◖	◖			O	I	I	I		

Runnin' the Changes: A 12 Bar in C

Playing a twelve bar using the notes of the chords is often called "running the changes" by jazz musicians. It's actually a jazz technique more than a blues technique. In this piece, try using some of the chords and rhythms that you just learned.

•		•	•	•	
1	2	3	3	repeat three more times
O	O	O	◖	

•		•	•	•	
2	3	4	5	repeat once more
I	I	O	◖	

•		•	•	•	
1	2	3	3	repeat once more
O	O	O	◖	

•		•	•	•		•		•	•	•	
3	4	5	6			2	3	4	5		
O	I	I	I			I	I	O	◖		

```
•        •   •   •          •       •   •   •
1   2   3   3              3   4   5   6
O   O   O   ]              O   I   I   I
```

Of course, you don't need to play each chord the same way each time (and shouldn't, once you've gotten the hang of it — boring). Break some of the notes into two parts, with emphasis on those downbeats — swing it!

Here's a twelve bar example, using more of the chord rhythms you just learned. In this verse, the last few beats that make up the turnaround are kind of a compromise between a G chord and a C chord. Practice that last line for a while, by itself. We might say that this turnaround consists of a C chord played in a downward direction, that emphasizes the G note of the C chord. However we could talk about it, it sounds great!

```
•        •   •   •          ••  •       •
1   2   3   3              3   3   2   1
O   O   O   ]              ]   O   O   O


•        •   •   •   •   •   •   •
1   2   3   3   3   2   1
O   O   O   ]   O   O   O


•        •   •   •          •       •   •       •
2   3   4   5              2   3   4   5   4   3
I   I   O   ]              I   I   O   ]   O   I


•        •   •   •   •   •   •   •
1   2   3   3   3   2   1
O   O   O   ]   O   O   O


•        •   •       •          •       •   •   •
3   4   5   6   5   4          2   3   4   5
O   I   I   I   I   I          I   I   O   ]


•        •   •   •       •       •   •   •
1   2   3   3   3   2   4   3   3   3
O   O   O   ]   O   O   O   O   ]   O
```

A Thrilling Twelve Bar

Here's an exciting variation on the standard twelve bar blues that's easy to play. In this variation, the bar of V chord and the bar of IV chord that follows it (in my two examples above, these would be the two bars on the next to the last line of each verse) are replaced by two different chords. The V chord is replaced by a V# (pronounced "five sharped") chord, and the IV chord is replaced by a V chord. Two of the best known songs that use a substitution of this kind are B. B. King's *The Thrill Is Gone* and George Gershwin's *Summertime* — two all-time classics!

This sounds complicated, but it is simple to play. Just substitute the G#7 and G7 chords that you've already practiced for the next to the last line in the verse on page 73. You can play the new line just once (since it is eight beats long, it will replace the original perfectly), or, if you like, repeat the new line three times before playing the original last line. Sounds fantastic, and jazzy!

```
  •     •   •   •           •       •   •   •
  3   4   5   6           3   4   5   6
  ◎   ⌷   ⌷   ⌷           O   I   I   I
```

More Chord Inversions

Here are a few of my favorite C7 inversions. Practice them as written, then apply some rhythm to them, then, when they feel really familiar, put them into a twelve bar. Also, feel free to substitute a higher or lower version of the same chords — I include some inversion examples of the C7 chord that usually begins on 5 Out, as well.

```
  2   3   3   1       2   3   3   4       3   3   1   2
  O   O   ⌷   O       O   O   ⌷   O       O   ⌷   O   O

  6   7   7   5       6   7   7   8       7   7   5   6
  O   O   ⌷   O       O   O   ⌷   O       O   ⌷   O   O
```

And here are a few F7 inversions.

3	4	5	6		5	2	3	4		5	6	7	8
I	O	◖	I		◖	I	I	O		◖	I	I	O

And a few G7 inversions.

3	4	1	2		4	5	6	7		4	5	2	3
O	I	I	I		I	I	I	O		I	I	I	O

See if you can create a twelve bar, using some different inversions and rhythms. Just use: four bars of C or C7 chord, then two bars of F or F7, then two more bars of C or C7, then one bar of G7, one bar of F or F7, and end it off with either two bars of C with an emphasis on a G note at the end, or one bar of C and one bar of G7. Presto: Instant twelve bar!

The Slidin' C Major Scale

And here's a slide exercise — not an easy one, but one that all good chro players must know. It's a way of playing the C Major Scale, using the slide to provide two of the notes that are normally played without it. Feels funny, but it's good practice! Compare it to the standard, no-slide, version, on page 59.

1	1	2	2	3	3	4	4	4	5	6	6	7	7	8	8
O	I	O	◎	O	I	I	◖	◖	I	O	◎	O	I	I	◖

And now, back to the blues for a while — the Real Blues Scale In D!

The Real Blues Scale in D

The Blues Scales are the very heart and soul of the blues, and of most jazz as well. If you've jumped to this page from earlier in the book (and I can hardly blame you for doing so), here's a mini-review of what you need to know to play the D Blues Scale, and the licks that follow.

The numbers tell you which hole to cover with your mouth. O means breathe Out, and I means breathe In, with the slide button not pressed. An outlined O or I means to breathe Out or In with the *slide button pressed*. Here's what the Blues Scale in D looks like. I'll break it into bite-size pieces in the next paragraphs. You can use either the 4 or the 5 Out note in this scale (they are the same note), but know which one you are using, or you'll have trouble finding the 5 In that comes next.

1	2	3	3	3	4 or 5	5
I	I	O	◎	I	O	I

Does that seem like a mouthful? If so, break the Blues Scale down into three more manageable parts. Practice playing each of the parts until it feels comfortable playing it both going up and going down. Begin with the first three notes of the scale, up then down. Play it in two ways — flowing smoothly from note to note, and then with a little "da" articulation (or even a "doo-wah" bend effect, if you studied page 47) on each note.

1	2	3		3	2	1
I	I	O		O	I	I

Now work that 3 hole: Out, Out with slide, and In.

3	3	3		3	3	3
O	◎	I		I	◎	O

Finish up with the last three notes. Try them both ways, using the 4 Out and using the 5 Out. Which seems easier? Decide which you're going to use, then try to be consistent, and use that note whenever you play the D Blues Scale.

3	4	5		5	4	3	or	3	5	5
I	O	I		I	O	I		I	O	I

When the three parts feel pretty familiar, return to the entire low end D Blues Scale, and play the whole thing, up and down. When you can do it in both directions (1 to 5, and 5 back to 1), try it continuously, going up, then back down without stopping. Hint: some beginners like to throw a strip of Scotch® tape over hole 6, just to help them know where they are.

1	2	3	3	3	4 or 5	5
I	I	O	◎	I	O	I

5	4 or 5	3	3	3	2	1
I	O	I	◎	O	I	I

Using the D Blues Scale in a Twelve Bar Blues

When you've learned this scale, you can use in a tremendous variety of ways, and they will all sound great! If you've got my tape, or other twelve bar backing music in the key of D, simply play the scale as a two bar (eight beat) lick by giving each note one beat, and ending with a beat of silence.

This lick will fit in perfectly six times (6 x 8 = 48) during the twelve bars (4 beats x 12 = 48) of a standard blues structure. Please remember to tap your foot once for each dot, to keep the beat. When you've got it down pat, try breaking each note into two parts by saying a "dada" tongue articulation, or adding a "doo-wah" bend type articulation.

•	•	•	•	•	•	•	•
1	2	3	3	3	4 or 5	5	
I	I	O	◎	I	O	I	

After you've done that for a while, make a sixteen beat (four bar) lick out of the up then down scale, and play it three times during each twelve bar verse. By the way, when playing D Blues Scale licks on the chromatic during a twelve bar, we often don't worry too much about changing our licks to fit each chord change. That's something that is done more when playing C blues on chro. So don't think too much, just get the feel of the D Blues Scale, and blow!

```
•    •    •    •    •         •         •  •
1    2    3    3    3      4 or 5       5
I    I    O    ◎    I         O         I


•         •         •  •  •  •  •
5       4 or 5      3  3  3  2  1
I         O         I  ◎  O  I  I
```

Creating Blues Scale Licks with Rhythm

In the above examples, each note got just one beat. And of course that isn't the most exciting rhythm around. So let's try applying some different rhythms to the D Blues Scale, to create licks. Here are some eight beat licks using the scale notes. After working on mine, make up some of your own. Use an articulation like "dada" to break any note into two pieces if you like, even though I didn't notate it.

```
••        •    •    •         •         •  •
1    2    3    3    3      4 or 5       5
I    I    O    ◎    I         O         I


•    •    •    •    ••                  •  •
1    2    3    3    3      4 or 5       5
I    I    O    ◎    I         O         I


••        •    •    ••                  •  •
1    2    3    3    3      4 or 5       5
I    I    O    ◎    I         O         I
```

And here are a couple of four beat Blues Scale licks. Swing the beat, that is, emphasize each downbeat (dot) by holding it a bit longer, and playing it a bit louder. Once again, try these, then make up some of your own. Notice that the last two feature three notes to the beat, which we might articulate more or less as a "diddeley diddeley dog" with an added beat of silence.

•	•	•		•		•
1	**2**	**3**	**3**	**3**	**4 or 5**	**5**
I	I	O	◎	I	O	I
did	de	ley	did	de	ley	dog

•	•	•	•	•		•	•
1	**2**	**3**	**3**	**3**	**4 or 5**	**5**	
I	I	O	◎	I	O	I	

•		•		•		•	•
5	**4 or 5**	**3**	**3**	**3**	**2**	**1**	
I	O	I	◎	O	I	I	

More Licks for the D Blues Scale

There's no law, fortunately for us, that says we have to play each note of the Blues Scale once, in order, when creating licks. So we can make up licks that jump around from note to note, or licks that repeat notes, or repeat parts of the scale. By doing this, we can compose literally millions of licks from the seven notes of the Blues Scale. Here are some licks that repeat a part of the Blues Scale. Try them smoothly, with one continuous breath, or choppily, with lots of articulation.

•	•	•	•	•	•	•	•	•	•	•	•
3	**3**	**3**	**3**	**3**	**3**	**3**	**3**	**3**	**3**	**2**	**1**
◎	O	◎	O	◎	O	◎	O	◎	O	I	I

As a variation of the above lick, try a fast flutter on the slide for the first four beats of the lick, as I indicate by outlining the number of the hole on which to do the flutter. So whenever you see a **number outlined** as well as the I or O, it means to do a very rapid (as fast as you can) in and out flutter of the slide button. Here are two versions of a flutter lick.

• • • •		•	•	•	•	• • • •		•		•	•	•
③		**3**	**2**	**1**		**③**		**3**		**2**	**1**	**1**
◎		O	I	I		◎		O		I	I	I

Here's another classic blues lick, often used as the last two bars (including turnaround) of a blues song.

```
  •         •   •       •   •       •   •   •
  3   3   2   3   3   2   3   3   2   1
  ◎   O   I   ◎   O   I   ◎   O   I   I
```

A Eight Bar Blues Scale Solo in D

This bluesy solo is reminiscent of the famous Cab Calloway song *Minnie The Moocher*. Try each line separately, and you won't find it too hard. Can you come up with variations on your own?

```
  •           •           •   •   •       •   •   •
  56    4 3 2 1           2   3   3   3   2   3
  I     I I I I           I   O   ◎   O   I   I


  •           •           •   •   •       •   •   •
  56    4 3 2 1           2   3   3   3   2   1
  I     I I I I           I   O   ◎   O   I   I


  •           •           •   •   •       •   •   •
  56    4 3 2 1           2   3   3   3   2   3   4
  I     I I I I           I   O   ◎   O   I   I   O


  •       •       •       •       •       •   •   •
  3   3   3   3   3   3   3   3   3   3   2   1
  ◎   O   ◎   O   ◎   O   ◎   O   ◎   O   I   I
```

The High End Blues Scale

As you may have guessed, the D Blues Scale can easily be played in the higher parts of the chro as well. If you have a twelve or sixteen holer, you can play the following scale. Do it going up, and down. If you only have an eight holer, don't worry — I'll tell you how to fudge it in a minute!

5	6	7	7	7	8 or 9	9
I	I	O	◎	I	O	I

Eight hole chro players can play up to the eight hole, then substitute a 1 In or 5 In for the final 9 In. It takes a bit of practice to make the jump to 5 In, but 1 In is easy, because there's no 0 In to confuse things!

5	6	7	7	7	8	1
I	I	O	◎	I	O	I

Naturally, all of the low end scale licks can easily be moved to the high end. Just substitute a 5 for every 1, a 6 for every 2, and a 7 for every 3. So a few of the low licks that I just gave you would look like this.

•		•		•		•		•		•	•	•
7	7	7	7	7	7	7	7	7	7	6	5	
◎	O	◎	O	◎	O	◎	O	◎	O	I	I	

•		•	•		•	•		•	•	•
7	7	6	7	7	6	7	7	6	5
◎	O	I	◎	O	I	◎	O	I	I

The Extended Blues Scale: Toots-Like

Once you've mastered that, you can play an extended Blues Scale. I'll notate it with 4 Out instead of 4 or 5 Out for convenience, but use whichever you're getting used to. Licks that cover a long distance like this are often called **runs** or **scale runs**. They sound even better than the shorter Blues Scale licks — jazzier — almost like something that Toots might have done when he was just starting to play! Do this one up and down.

1	2	3	3	3	4	5	6	7	7	7	8	9 or 1
I	I	O	◎	I	O	I	I	O	◎	I	O	I

Here's one of my favorite long runs.

		•			•			•			•
1	2	3	3	3	4	5	6	7	7	7	8
I	I	O	◎	I	O	I	I	O	◎	I	O

•		•		•	•
7	7	7	6	5	5	5
I	◎	O	I	I	O	I

I threw in a few 1 Out notes on these next two runs. Why does 1 Out work? Because it's the same as 4 Out or 8 Out, and thus a perfectly good D Blues Scale note. Play a couple of nice jumping around D Blues Scales like these, by jumping to a lower note near the end.

1	2	3	3	3	1	1		5	6	7	7	7	4	5
I	I	O	◎	I	O	I		I	I	O	◎	I	O	I

Make some runs up that use the 1 Out note after you play these.

•		•		•		•		•		•	•	•
7	7	6	5	4	3	3	3	2	1	1	1	2	1	1	1
◎	O	I	I	O	I	◎	O	I	I	O	I	I	I	O	I

•	•		•		•		•		•		•
5	6	7	7	7	6	5	4	3	3	3	2	1
I	I	O	◎	O	I	I	O	I	◎	O	I	I

Some Extended Blues Scale Solos in D

Put them together for a hot eight bar solo, like this.

•	•		•		•		•		•		•		•
5	6	7	7	7	6	5	4	3	3	3	2	1	
I	I	O	◎	O	I	I	O	I	◎	O	I	I	

•	•		•		•		•		•		•		•
5	6	7	7	7	6	5	4	3	3	3	3		
I	I	O	◎	O	I	I	O	I	◎	O	I		

•	•		•		•		•		•		•		•
5	6	7	7	7	6	5	4	3	3	3	2	1	
I	I	O	◎	O	I	I	O	I	◎	O	I	I	

•		•		•		•		•		•	•	•
7	7	6	5	4	3	3	3	2	1	1	1	2	1	1	1
◎	O	I	I	O	I	◎	O	I	I	O	I	I	I	O	I

Or try them (with a few changes for the third and fifth lines to fit the IV and V chords by emphasizing the notes 7 Out during the IV and 7 In during the V) as a twelve bar solo: This isn't an easy blues, especially when you have to turn the page in the middle! But it's worth picking out.

•	•		•		•		•		•		•		•
5	6	7	7	7	6	5	4	3	3	3	2	1	
I	I	O	◎	O	I	I	O	I	◎	O	I	I	

•	•		•		•		•		•		•
5	6	7	7	7	6	5	4	3	3	3	2	1
I	I	O	◎	O	I	I	O	I	◎	O	I	I

•	•		•		•			•	•		•
7	6	5	7	7	6		7	6	5	7
O	I	I	O	O	I		O	I	I	O

```
 •    •      •      •      •      •      •         •
 5    6    7    7    7    6    5    4    3    3    3    2    1
 I    I    O    ◎    O    I    I    O    I    ◎    O    I    I

 •    •      •      •           •    •         •    •
 7    7    7    8    7    6         7    6    5    7
 I    O    I    O    I    I         O    I    I    O

 •         •         •         •              •      •    •    •
 7    7    6    5    4    3    3    3    2    1    1    1    2    1    1    1
 ◎    O    I    I    O    I    ◎    O    I    I    O    I    I    I    O    I
```

The possibilities are endless — an entire book could easily be filled with just D Blues Scale licks and solos. After working with these examples, I hope that you'll be able to begin creating your own D Blues Scales songs and improvisations.

The C Blues Scale

The only reason that the C Blues Scale is harder than the D Blues Scale is that it requires more slide button work. But I hope that by now, you're feeling pretty comfortable with the slide button, since (as you may have already noticed with the D Blues Scale) the slide use is the most fun part of the scale! Here's the low end C Blues Scale. I'm not going to break it into parts as I did with the D, so give it a try now, slowly and carefully, while looking at the notation. Do it up, then do it down, then do it up and down, with just enough rhythm to make it a tasty run.

```
 1    1    2    2    3    3    4
 O    ◖    I    ◖    O    ◖    O

                     4    3    3    2    2    1    1
                     O    ◖    O    ◖    I    ◖    O

 •         •         •         •         •         •    •
 1    1    2    2    3    3    4    3    3    2    2    1    1
 O    ◖    I    ◖    O    ◖    O    ◖    O    ◖    O    ◖    I    ◖    O
```

Higher End C Blues Scales

Once you feel comfortable with the low end C Blues Scale, try these higher ones, depending on what size harp you have. If you have a sixteen holer, you can actually do a wonderful run that uses all sixteen holes, just by playing one long, continuous C Blues Scale from bottom to top! As with the D Blues Scale, be careful that you don't get the 4 and 5 Out holes mixed up (or the 8 and 9 Out holes), or you won't know where you are when you need to go to the next note.

```
5    5    6    6    7    7    8
O    ◖    I    ◖    O    ◖    O
```

```
                    9    9    10   10   11   11   12
                    O    ◖    I    ◖    O    ◖    O
```

The Extended C Blues Scale and Solos

Just as we did with the D Blues Scale, we can play longer runs by combining a lower and a higher C Blues Scale. Begin with this one. After you've learned to play it upwards, play it down. I'll throw a bit of rhythm onto each to form one sixteen and one eight beat run, but ignore the rhythm dots until you can hit the notes correctly.

```
••   ••        •    •    •    •    ••   •    •    •    •    •    •
1    1    2    2    3    3    4    5    6    6    7    7    8
O    ◖    I    ◖    O    ◖    O    ◖    I    ◖    O    ◖    O
```

```
•              •              •              •              •        • • •
8    7    7    6    6    5    4    3    3    2    2    1    1
O    ◖    O    ◖    I    ◖    O    ◖    O    ◖    I    ◖    O
```

If you like (and if you have a bigger harp), work on your high end C Blues Scale, and simply attach it onto the lower scales for a humongously long run. Play it from right to left, too, if you dare.

```
  •           •           •           •
  1   1   2   2   3   3   4   5   6   6   7   7
  O   ]   I   ]   O   ]   O   ]   I   ]   O   ]

                  •           •               •           •
                  8   9   10  10  11  11  12
                  O   ]   I   ]   O   ]   O
```

Jamming With the C Blues Scale

Just as with the D Blues Scale, we can simply play the C Blues Scale along with a C Twelve Bar Blues backing, and it will sound fine. We can repeat any two bar (eight beat) licks six times to fill up our twelve bars, or repeat any four bar (sixteen beat) licks three times. We don't, of course, have to repeat the same lick either. We can use any combination of licks that will fill the 48 beats of a standard blues verse, as I demonstrate on the tape.

But unlike the D Blues Scale, when jamming with the C Blues Scales, chromatic harpists usually try to make their runs, licks, and solos change to fit the chords of the background music.

In a certain way, jamming with the C Blues Scale can be like a compromise between just playing the C Blues Scale during a blues twelve bar, and the arpeggiated chord blues in C that you've already played. How's that? Well, when you just play the C Blues Scale during a jamm, you are not changing the notes at all to fit the chords. In the arpeggiated blues, the chords that are playing in the background music determine exactly which notes you must play.

Here's an example of a Blues in C in which I use lots of C Blues Scale notes throughout the verse, but I make sure to emphasize lots of F notes (2 In or 6 In) during the F chords, and G notes (3 Out or 7 Out) during the G chord. Notice the classic turnaround — you'll hear it a lot, if you listen to blues.

```
 •       •   •   •   •   •   •   •   •   •       •   •  •••
 1   1   1   2   2   3   3   4       5   4   3   3       1
 O   O   ]   I   ]   O   ]   O       ]   O   ]   O       O
```

2	2	1	1	2	2	1		1	1	2	2		3
I	I	▯	O	I	I	▯		O	▯	I	▯		O

3	3	3	3		2	2	1
O	O	▯	O		I	I	▯

1	1	1	1	2	2	2	2	3	2	2	3
O	O	▯	▯	I	I	▯	▯	O	I	▯	O

But to really play exciting blues, it's important to understand two more things: the Expanded Blues Scale, and the concept of using multiple Blues Scales in a single verse.

The Expanded Blues Scale

The Expanded Blues Scale is not a scale that we usually play — it's almost more like an idea than a scale. It just means that there are notes that we often use when playing blues, notes that aren't in the Blues Scale, but that sound right if they are sprinkled in amongst lots of Blues Scale notes. Here is the Expanded Blues Scale in C. I've made the four "extra" notes less bold. As you may have noticed, these notes happen to be the notes of the C Major Scale that are not usually included in the C Blues Scale.

C	D	D#	E	F	F#	G	A	A#	B	C
1	1	1	2	2	2	3	3	4	4	4
O	I	▯	O	I	▯	O	I	▯	I	O

You can practice playing this scale if you like — be my guest. But what is mostly important is to understand that it is okay to use non-Blues Scale notes when playing the blues. You'll see plenty of these notes in the next songs.

The Classic Blues Boogie Woogie in C

The boogie woogie is a special type of blues music. Born in the red light districts of the Mississippi Delta region before the turn of the century, it is probably based on the left hand patterns played by long dead pianists. This is the standard, classic, boogie woogie. It has been used as a bassline or jumping-off point for literally countless blues, jazz, and rock tunes. Compare it to the chart on page 50 — you'll see that it is a twelve bar blues structure. Here's a simple version, with only one note per beat.

```
•   •   •   •   •   •   •   •
1   2   3   3   3   3   3   2
O   O   O   I   I   I   O   O


•   •   •   •   •   •   •   •
1   2   3   3   3   3   3   2
O   O   O   I   I   I   O   O


•   •   •   •   •   •   •   •
2   3   4   5   5   5   4   3
I   I   O   I   I   I   O   I


•   •   •   •   •   •   •   •
1   2   3   3   3   3   3   2
O   O   O   I   I   I   O   O


•   •   •   •       •   •   •   •
3   4   5   6       2   3   4   5
O   I   I   O       I   I   O   I


•   •   •   •   •       •   •   •
1   2   3   3   3   3   3   3
O   O   O   I   I   I   O   O
```

But the true boogie woogie is usually played "eight to the bar", that is, with eight notes in each four beat bar. Play it with a swingin' feel! Emphasize those downbeats!

•		•		•		•		•		•		•		•	
1	1	2	2	3	3	3	3	3	3	3	3	3	3	2	2
O	O	O	O	O	O	I	I	0	0	I	I	O	O	O	O

•		•		•		•		•		•		•		•	
1	1	2	2	3	3	3	3	3	3	3	3	3	3	2	2
O	O	O	O	O	O	I	I	0	0	I	I	O	O	O	O

•		•		•		•		•		•		•		•	
2	2	3	3	4	4	5	5	5	5	5	5	4	4	3	3
I	I	I	I	O	O	I	I	0	0	I	I	O	O	I	I

•		•		•		•		•		•		•		•	
1	1	2	2	3		3	3	3	3	3	3	3	3	2	2
O	O	O	O	O		I	I	0	0	I	I	O	O	O	O

•		•		•		•		•		•		•		•	
3	3	4	4	5	5	6	5		2	2	3	3	4	4	5	5
O	O	I	I	I	I	O	I		I	I	I	I	O	O	I	O

•		•		•		•		•		•		•		•	
1	1	2	2	3	3	3	3	4	3	3	3
O	O	O	O	O	O	I	I	O	0	O	O

Improvising on the Boogie Woogie in C

Playing the boogie woogie as it is written is all very well, but the real fun lies in adding various Blues Scale notes to make it sound better. In this version, I vary the timing, add a few notes, and a classic boogie woogie turnaround. I'll get wild, later.

```
 •        •   •   •   •   •   •   •
 1   1   2   3   3   3   3   3   2
 O   O   O   O   I   ◖   I   O   O


 •        •   •   •   •   •   •   •
 1   1   2   3   3   4   3   3   3   3
 O   O   O   O   I   O   ◖   O   ◖   O


 •   •   •   •   •   •           •   •
 2   3   4   5   5   5   5   5   4   3
 I   I   O   I   ◖   I   ◖   I   O   I


 •        •   •   •   •   •       •       •
 1   1   2   3   3   3   4   5   6   5   4
 O   O   O   O   I   ◖   O   I   O   I   O


 •   •        •   •       •       •       •   •
 3   4   5   6   7   7   8   7   7   6   5   3
 O   I   I   I   O   I   I   I   O   O   I   O


 •        •       •       •       •       •   •   •
 4   4   3   3   3   3   3   3   3   2   2   3
 O   O   ◖   ◖   I   I   ◎   ◎   O   I   ◖   O
```

Is it later yet? Here's a boogie woogie as I might play it in a slightly whimsical mood.
Why do I use the notes that I use? Because they seemed right at the moment! And it works!

```
 •     •  •  •  •  •  •  •
 1  1  2  3  3  3  3  3  2
 O  O  O  O  I  I  I  O  O

 •  •     •     •     •     •  •  •
 1  6  4  3  3     4  6  4  3  3
 O  O  O  I  O     O  O  O  I  O

 •  •     •     •        •     •  •  •
 2  6  5  5  6     7  7  7  6  5
 I  I  O  I  I     O  ◎  O  I  I

 •  •     •     •        •     •  •     •
 1  6  4  3  4     5  6  7  7  8  7  7
 O  O  O  I  O     I  O  O  I  O  I  O

 •     •     •     •     •     •  •     •
 3  3  2  1  2  3     3  4  5  4  3  3  3  3
 O  O  I  I  I  O     I  I  I  I  O  O  I  O

 •  •     •     •        •     •  •     •
 4  6  3  3  5     5  6  5  4  3
 O  O  O  I  O     I  O  I  O  O
```

A Few More Blues Scales: F and G

As I mentioned before, sometimes it's fun to use multiple Blues Scales within a single
song. Usually, when we do this, we use the Blues Scale that is the same as the chord that
is playing. So when playing a Twelve Bar Blues in C, with its C, F, and G chords, we might
also use an F Blues Scale during the F chord parts, and a G Blues Scale during the G parts,
in addition to the C Blues Scale which we use during the C chords.

Here is the F Blues Scale followed by the G Blues Scale. Easy? Not particularly. But interesting to use, for a jazzy effect.

F	G#	A#	B	C	D#	F		G	A#	C	C#	D	F	G
2	3	3	4	5	5	6		3	3	4	5	5	6	7
I	◎	]	I	O	]	I		O	]	O	◎	I	I	O

Using C, F, and G Blues Scales Together

The simplest way to use these scales together in a twelve bar structure in C is to play each as an eight beat lick. Often, when using this method of improvising, we will hold the V chord (G) for two bars instead of one, and omit the last bar of IV chord (F). So use the C scale twice, then F once, then C again once, then G once, then C again, like this.

·	·	·	·	·	·	·	·		·	·	·	·	·	·	·	·	·
1	1	2	2	3	3	4			1	1	2	2	3	3	4		
O	]	I	]	O	]	O			O	]	I	]	O	]	O		

·	·	·	·	·	·	·	·
2	3	3	4	5	5	6	
I	◎	]	I	O	]	I	

·	·	·	·	·	·	·	·
1	1	2	2	3	3	4	
O	]	I	]	O	]	O	

·	·	·	·	·	·	·	·	·
3	3	4	5	5	6	7		
O	]	O	◎	I	I	O		

·	·	·	·	·	·	·	·	·
1	1	2	2	3	3	4		
O	]	I	]	O	]	O		

Please feel free to add some rhythm, or create F and G licks of your own by choosing various notes from the F and G Blues Scales, just as we've done with the D and C Blues Scales.

Slightly in the Style of Stevie

We chromatic harmonica players are lucky — one of the world's most talented musicians favors our instrument of choice. I'm talking, as you may have already guessed, about Stevie Wonder. His style of playing is so varied that it's difficult to describe, so I'm tempted merely to advise you to purchase as many of his numerous recordings as you can find, and study them.

As far as chord structures go, although he occasionally plays in a twelve bar structure, much of his playing is of structures that he has composed, so the only advice I can give on that is to listen well.

But there are certain elements in his playing that I can discuss which may be helpful. For instance, Stevie (as I will familiarly presume to call him), begins many of his notes with a bending effect. Some of his notes start with a powerful "doo-wah", as described in the bending section on page 47. Others have just a faint touch of bentness in the way he articulates. He also makes much use of his slide button, sometimes slowly, sometimes in a fast but beautifully controlled flutter.

It would be presumptuous of me to offer you licks that were supposed to be in Stevie's style. I don't believe that anyone can really play his style, but he himself. However, I'd like to present a few of my own creations, meant as a tribute to the man and his music, which may faintly illustrate some of the techniques that he uses. Play this lick first as a sixteen beat lick.

•	•		•		•	•		•		•	
5	5	5	5	5		5	5	5	5	5	
◖	I	◖	I	O		◖	I	◖	I	O	

•	•		•	•	•	•	•	•
5	5	5	5	5	5	8		
◖	I	◖	I	O	O	O		

Now add a few flourishes and try speeding it up to eight.

•			•			•			•		
5	5	5	5	5	3		5	5	5	5	5	3
◖	I	◖	I	O	I		◖	I	◖	I	O	I

•			•		•		•	
5	5	5	5	5	3	8		
◖	I	◖	I	O	I	O		

Tribute to Stevie: A Twelve Bar

Take a combination of the first lick and the second, and carry it through an entire twelve bar. Although I have doubled the number of dots to make it easier to read, I mean this to be a twelve bar rather than a twenty four bar. So, if you like, tap your foot on every other dot instead of every dot, once you've gotten the hang of it.

```
•   •         •   •         •   •               •   •
5   5   5   5   5   3       5   5   5   5   5   3
▯   I   ▯   I   O   I       ▯   I   ▯   I   O   I


•   •         •   •   •         •   •   •
5   5   5   5   5   3   5
▯   I   ▯   I   O   I   O


•   •         •   •         •   •               •   •
5   5   5   5   5   3       5   5   5   5   5   3
▯   I   ▯   I   O   I       ▯   I   ▯   I   O   I


•   •         •   •         •       •   •   •
5   5   5   5   5   3       5
▯   I   ▯   I   O   I       O


•   •         •   •         •   •               •   •
3   3   3   3   2   1       3   3   3   3   2   1
◎   O   ◎   O   I   I       ◎   O   ◎   O   I   I


•   •         •   •         •       •   •   •
3   3   3   3   2   1       6
◎   O   ◎   O   I   I       I


•   •         •   •         •   •               •   •
5   5   5   5   5   3       5   5   5   5   5   3
▯   I   ▯   I   O   I       ▯   I   ▯   I   O   I
```

```
 •   •        •   •        •        •    •    •
 5   5   5   5   5   3     5
 ◖   I   ◖   I   O   I     O


 •   •        •   •        •    •         •    •
 3   3   3   3   3   2     3    3    3    3    2    1
 ◖   I   ◖   I   O   O     ◎    O    ◎    O    I    I


 •   •        •   •        •        •    •    •
 5   5   5   5   5   3     8
 ◖   I   ◖   I   O   I     O
```

Lazy Bends:　A Short Solo

This riff illustrates the use of bending effects combined with slide use. I'll indicate a bend with a small "b" next to the note that is meant to be bent. Use the "doo-wah" articulation that I've described on all notes with a small b.

```
 •   •        •   •        • • •        •
 6   6   6   6   5   4     5
 ◎b  O   ◎   O   I   I     Ib


 •   •        •   •        • • •        •
 6   6   6   6   5   4     3
 ◎b  O   ◎   O   I   I     Ib


 •   •        •   •        •    •    •    •
 6   6   6   6   5   4     5    6
 ◎b  O   ◎   O   I   I     Ib   I


 •        •        •        •    •    •    •    •
 7   7   6   5   5   5   5   6
 ◎b  O   I   Ib  O   Ib  O   Ib
```

Perhaps the best way to learn more about Stevie's style is to study one of his songs in depth. One of my favorites, and a piece that demonstrates many of his techniques, is the beautiful *Isn't She Lovely*. Since it is in the key of E, if you practice your E Major Scale and E Blues Scale, you'll be able to pick out both the melody of the song (that is, the tune that goes with the words) and create improvisations. Here's how to play an E Major Scale, followed by an E Blues Scale.

E Major Scale

E	F#	G#	A	B	C#	D#	E
2	2	3	3	4	4	5	6
O	◗	◎	I	I	◎	◗	O

E Blues Scale

E	G	A	A#	B	D	E
2	3	3	3	4	5	6
O	O	I	◗	I	I	O

Slightly in the Style of Toots

Another chromatic player who must rank at the top of anybody's list is Toots Thielemans. The sensitivity of his playing, and his knowledge of just which note to use where make him one of the most sought-after studio players of our time, and his sincerity and dignity in concert make his appearances most memorable.

As with Stevie, I would never try to play in Toots' style. However, I can give you a few hints that may help you to understand what he is doing in some of his songs that you may listen to. Practicing the various Blues Scale runs from pages 82 and 85 will give you some of the same theoretical underpinnings that he uses in his blues and ballad work.

Toots will often begin a note bent (usually an In note with the slide pressed), then slowly unbend it (the "doo-wah" again) and let the slide out just as the note reaches its unbent state. He also often applies a very gentle vibrato to a note (see page 47).

The following lick has an entire series of such notes: try to begin each one bent, then unbend it and release the slide before moving on to the next note. When you begin to feel comfortable doing this, go back to the runs mentioned above, and apply the same technique to some of the appropriate notes. Which are they? That's up to you, but look for In notes with the slide pressed. Here's your exercise, plus a nice little run to practice on.

•	•	•	•	•	•	•	•	•	•
7	7	6	6	5	5		7	7	6	6	5	5
▯b	▯	▯b	▯	▯b	▯		▯b	▯	▯b	▯	▯b	▯

•	•	•	•	•	•	•	•
7	7	6	6	5	5	4	4	3	3	2	2	1	1
▯b	▯	▯b	▯	▯b	▯	▯b	▯	▯b	▯	▯b	▯	▯b	▯

•	•	•	••	•	•	•	•	••	•
8	7	7	6	6	5	4	3	3	2	2	1
O	▯	O	▯b	▯	▯	O	▯	O	▯b	▯	▯

•	•	•	••	•	•	•••••
1	1	2	2	2	1	1
O	▯	▯	▯b	▯	▯	O

As I suggested with Stevie, if you really want to learn about Toots's style, listen to him! One of my favorite pieces for playing along with is the Billy Joel song *Leave A Tender Moment Alone*, with chro work by Toots.

It's in the key of B flat, so if you practice the Bb Major Scale, and Bb Blues Scale written below, you'll be able to jamm along, even though the chord structure of the song is quite complicated.

B flat Major Scale

Bb	C	D	D#	F	G	A	Bb
3	4	5	5	6	7	7	7
〗	O	I	〗	I	O	I	〗

B flat Blues Scale

Bb	C#	D#	E	F	G#	Bb
3	5	5	6	6	7	7
〗	◎	〗	O	I	◎	〗

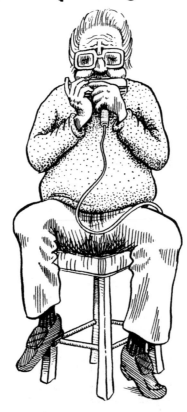

Appendix A: Music Theory for the "Musically Insecure"

You might call this chapter "everything you always wanted to know about music but were afraid to ask". It's a simplified overview of the physics of sound, and the history and theory of music.

Good Vibrations

Imagine a bumblebee that has suffered the indignity of falling into a swimming pool.

Its wings vibrate, and these vibrations make tiny waves in the water. These waves make a leaf near the edge of the pool vibrate at the same speed as the bee's wings are vibrating.

Whenever anything vibrates, it creates additional vibrations that spread through the air. Sometimes what is vibrating is obvious, like the head of a drum or the wings of a mosquito or a guitar string.

Sometimes what vibrates is not so obvious, like the tiny metal reeds that move swiftly back and forth inside the covers of our chromatic.

The speed of any of these vibrations will vary, depending on what is vibrating. The drum head vibrates at a low speed, and sends big, slow waves through the air. The mosquito's wings vibrate at a very high speed, and send tiny, fast waves through the air. The vibratory speed of the reeds depend on the size of the reed. The larger, heavier reeds in the low end of our chros vibrate more slowly, and the smaller, lighter reeds in the high end vibrate more rapidly. But no matter the speed of the vibrations, the vibrations radiate out into the air, and make the air itself vibrate.

Air, Ear, and Brain

When vibrations travelling in the air reach our eardrums, our eardrums then vibrate at the same speed as whatever is vibrating, just like the bee's wings made the leaf vibrate.

A complicated set of bones, organs, and nerves connect our eardrums to the brain. They convey messages which let the brain know how fast the eardrums are vibrating. When our eardrums are vibrating slowly, our brain interprets this message as what we call a low sound. When our eardrums are vibrating quickly, our brain interprets this message as what we call a high sound. Thus hearing is an interaction taking place amongst the vibrations in the air, the ear, and the brain.

Notes and Octave

Let's choose a particular vibrational speed which produces a sound, like 200 vibrations per second (vps), for example.

If we compare this particular sound, (which can also be called a note) with the note

If we compare this particular sound, (which can also be called a note) with the note produced by 400 vps (exactly twice as fast), we'll find that the two sounds seem remarkable alike, although the faster vibration sound is obviously higher. If we double the speed of vibration once again (800 vps), we find that all three sounds (200 vps, 400 vps and 800 vps) bear a great similarity to each other. Likewise the sounds produced by 300 vps, 600 vps and 1200 vps sound alike, and so on.

Doubling the speed of vibration of a particular sound will always produce a new sound that seems to repeat the sound quality of the first one, only higher. We call these similar notes **octave notes.** We can also call the distance between two of these octave notes one octave.

As you may have already guessed, the chromatic harmonica is full of octave notes. 1 Out, 4 and 5 Out, 8 and 9 Out, and 12 Out are octave notes — they are all C notes (more about letter names later), and all sound basically the same, even though some are lower and some are higher. Scientists have shown that if you train a dog to salivate when he hears a low C note (like a 1 Out), he will also salivate when he hears a 4 Out or 8 Out (higher C notes)!

Pythagoras

2500 years ago the Greek metaphysician Pythagoras turned his brilliant mind to the question of why a bow string produces different sounds when stretched to different degrees. He soon discovered that lengths of string stretched between two points with equal tension would produce varying sounds depending on the length of the string.

Pythagoras began to experiment with the sounds produced by plucking different lengths of string. He noticed that if he plucked two strings simultaneously when one was exactly half as long as the other, they would both produce sounds that some-how seemed very similar, even though the shorter string made a sound that was clearly higher.

Modern musicians now know that the "half-as-long" string was vibrating exactly twice as fast as the longer string, and thus the shorter string was producing an octave note which sounded very much like the longer string's original note. But the vibrational nature of sound was not discovered until nearly 1700 A.D., so Pythagoras had only the relative lengths of the strings, and the evidence of his own ears, to base his research on.

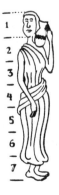

The Ancient Greeks and Their Ratios

The ancient Greeks were heavily into ratios. They used them in their mathematics, in their architecture, and in their art. For example, the ratio of a male statue's neck to its wrist was always 2 to 1, and the ratio of the height of the head to the length of the body was 7 to 1. So it was natural for Pythagoras to want to apply ratios to his musical musings.

He reasoned that if the mathematical ratio of 2 to 1 (one string twice as long as the other) would produce two sounds that seemed so similar, perhaps other simple ratios like 3 to 2 or 4 to 3 could be applied to the lengths of vibrating strings to produce more sounds that somehow "related well" to each other.

The Chromatic Scale

Pythagoras continued his experimentation. He used a variety of mathematical ratios (like 5 to 4, 3 to 2, 4 to 3, etc.) to divide up the musical distance between two octave notes into smaller sections. Eventually he ended up by dividing each octave into 12 equal sections.

We call this process of breaking up the octave distance into a number of smaller pieces "creating a scale". The word scale refers to a particular way of dividing that octave distance into pieces. Pythagoras' 12 note division (actually a 13 note division if you count the first and last note of the scale, which are really the "same" notes, one octave apart) is still the basic scale used by most of our Western civilization's music and musical instruments. It is called the chromatic scale. We call our harmonica a chromatic harmonica, because it plays all the notes of the chromatic scale.

You can begin a chromatic scales on any note of a piano, and just play up thirteen black and white notes (including the beginning and ending notes). After I've told you about note names, I'll give you two examples of chromatic scales, marked off by the upper and lower brackets in the picture below. One begins and ends on an E note, the other on a Bb (B flat) note.

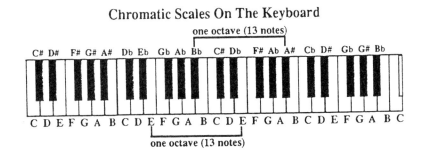

Chromatic Scales On The Keyboard

Why did Pythagoras do it just this way? No one today knows for sure, but a quick look at the piano keyboard (which usually contains seven and one third chromatic scales next to each other) will clearly show that Pythagoras' 12 note octave division, has stood the test of time!

The Letter Names of Notes: Sharps (#) and Flats (b)

By the late middle ages each piano note had been assigned a letter name. Each white note is indicated by a simple letter (C - D - E - F - G - A - B - C), but each black note has two names.

One letter name is called a **sharp** name. Sharp means "higher than". The sharp name tells us which white key the black key is a little bit higher than. So the black key named "A sharp" is the black key a little bit higher than A. Sometimes instead of "sharp", we use the symbol **#.**

The other letter name is called a **flat** name. Flat means "lower than". The flat name tells us which white key the black key is a little bit lower than. So the black key named "B flat" is the black key a little bit lower than B. Sometimes instead of the word "flat", we use the symbol **b.**

You can see that A sharp and B flat are exactly the same note. Please look at the picture of a piano with all the letter names for white and black notes (both # and b).

Letter note names are specific. That is, the note C refers to a note that is vibrating at a specific speed, or any note vibrating twice or half that fast. If someone says C, or Bb, or G#, we can immediately put our finger on that note, without needing any more information.

When we choose a note to begin a scale on, the name of that beginning note is then the **key** of that scale. So, for instance, any scale beginning and ending on the note D is called a D Scale, or a Scale in the key of D.

Other Types of Note Names: Solmi and Roman

Since we're not piano players, with lots of notes to look at, another way of naming notes, called solmization, may be more useful for our purposes. In solmization, each note of the chromatic scale is given a syllable name, like this.

DO di RE ri ME FA fi SO si LA li TI DO

Solmi names are not as specific as letter names. They do not refer to particular notes, but they do accurately describe the relationship between notes. A di is always one note up from a DO on the piano for instance, and a si always six up from a RE (counting black and white keys as exactly the same). Thus the third note of the E chromatic scale and the third note of the Bb chromatic scale indicated by brackets in the picture of a piano above are called by the same solmi name: RE.

All DO notes are exactly one octave apart, and sound very similar to each other. All RE notes are one octave apart, and every RE sounds similar to every other RE. This picture may help to illustrate for you the repeated nature of the chromatic scale.

There is one other common way of referring to notes. It is very similar to the solmi names, but instead of being given a syllable, each note of the chromatic scale is given a roman numeral. Since only seven Roman numerals are used, sharp and flat signs are added to make the twelve note names needed for a chromatic scale. This is how the Solmi and Roman note names compare to each other. Since any note with a sharp name also has a flat name, I'll put the sharp name on top, and the flat name on the bottom. Since the slide button on a chromatic harp raises (or sharps) a note when it is pressed, I like to use sharp names instead of flat names whenever possible.

DO	di	RE	ri	ME	FA	fi	SO	si	LA	li	TI	DO
I	I#	II	II#	III	IV	IV#	V	V#	VI	VI#	VII	I
	bII		bIII			bV		bVI		bVII		

The Major Scale, the Minor Scale, and the Blues Scale

Many different types of scales exist, and each scale is used to create a different kind of music. As I said earlier, we might consider a scale to be a kind of "musical alphabet". By using various combinations of the 26 letters of the English alphabet we create English words, sentences, paragraphs and books. By using the letters of the Russian alphabet we create Russian words, sentences and long dreary novels. Likewise, the notes of any particular culture's scale, be it a Greek scale, a Chinese scale, or a Martian scale, can be put together in various combinations to create music with a sound characteristic of that culture.

Although Pythagoras' Chromatic scale (below) is the basis of Western civilization's music, it is rarely used in its complete 12 note form. Instead, certain notes are chosen from it (usually six or seven) to form less complex new scales.

By the Middle Ages, two of these new scales had become far more popular than any of the others that had been tried. These two most popular scales were named the Major and Minor scales. Each has eight notes. But the way that each scale's octave distance is broken up is different. Thus the Major and Minor scales have a very different musical "feel" from each other.

The Major Scale eventually evolved as the basis for much of Northern and Western Europe's music. We might call it the "musical alphabet" for most German and English classical music, and some folk music. It tends to have a strong, brassy, bouncy feel to it. Even random playing of the major scale notes sounds good to us — because these notes are the most basic building blocks of our American musical heritage.

Do	RE	ME	FA	SO	LA	TI	DO
I	II	III	IV	V	VI	VII	I

The Minor scale evolved as the basis for much of Eastern Europe's music. It has a more plaintive or wistful quality, and we might consider it to be the alphabet of most Gypsy and Yiddish music, and some folk music as well.

DO	RE	ri	FA	SO	si	li	DO
I	II	II#	IV	V	V#	VI#	I

There is one more musical alphabet we must learn about: The Afro - American Blues Scale. Its seven notes always sound "bluesy" when played together in any combination. Blues Scale notes are traditionally referred to by their "flat" names rather than their "sharp" names, so I have included the Roman numerals indicating the bIII, bV, and bVII notes. Verbally, blues musicians call these the "flatted third", "flatted fifth", and "flatted seventh" notes.

DO		ri	FA	fi	So		li		DO
I		II#	IV	IV#	V		VI#		I
		bIII		bV			bVII		

Comparing C Chromatic, Major, Minor and Blues Scales

Although there are a number of ways to play these scales, using the duplicated notes on the chromatic, for simplicities sake I will just write them out in the way that I find easiest to play them. I've lined them up so that you can see the way they compare to each other, which notes are the same, and which notes are different.

"C" Chromatic:	C	C#	D	D#	E	F	F#	G	G#	A	A#	B	C
	1	1	1	1	2	2	2	3	3	3	3	4	4
	O	◎	I	◖	O	I	◖	O	◎	I	◖	I	O

"C" Major:	C		D		E	F		G		A		B	C
	1		1		2	2		3		3		4	4
	O		I		O	I		O		I		I	O

"C" Blues:	C			D#		F	F#	G			A#		C
	1			1		2	2	3			3		4
	O			◖		I	◖	O			◖		O

"C" Minor:	C		D	D#		F		G	G#		A#		C
	1		1	1		2		3	3		3		4
	O		I	◖		I		O	◎		◖		O

A Few More Blues Scales

Here are a few more Blues Scales in the form of a chart, with the notes to emphasize during the IV and V chords *italicized* (they are the notes of each scale under the numerals I, IV, and V).

To create a twelve bar solo in these different keys, simply use any and all of the notes of the scale during the I chord parts of the verse. Emphasize the IV note during the IV chords, and emphasize the V note during the V chords. And if you've gotten this far, you'll be able to pick out licks and runs in A, Bb, or E, once you've practiced these Blues Scales.

Key	*I*		*IV*		*V*		
	A	C	*D*	D#	*E*	G	A
A	3	4	5	5	6	7	7
	I	O	I	▮	O	O	I
	Bb	C#	*D#*	E	*F*	G#	Bb
Bb	3	5	5	6	6	7	7
	◖	◎	◖	O	I	◎	◖
	E	G	*A*	A#	*B*	D	E
E	2	3	3	3	4	5	6
	O	O	I	◖	I	I	O

About Chords

Chords, as I said in the main part of the book, are notes that sound right together. Most chords are made up of three or four notes, and there are only two types of chords that are really included in this book, the Major Chords, and the Major Seventh or Seventh Chords.

Major Chords, like the C, F, and G that we use a lot, are always made up in the same way. Once you decide the key of the chord (that is, what note you are going to start the chord on), you know exactly what notes will be in the chord. You will have the note that it starts on, plus the third note of the Major Scale in that key, plus the fifth note of the Major Scale in that key.

For example, a C Major Chord will always start on C, then have an E and a G, because E and G are the third and fifth notes of the C Major Scale (C D E F G A B C).

Seventh Chords always have the same three notes as a Major Chord, plus the note which is in between the sixth and seventh note of that chord's Major Scale. To form a C7 chord, we would take the notes of a C Major Chord C, E, and G. Then we would add the Bb or A# note, since it is the note between the sixth (A) and seventh (B) note of the C Major Scale. Knowing about chords may add to your enjoyment when you play the arpeggiated chord blues!

Reading Standard Notation: A Beginning

Knowing how to read standard musical notation is a plus for any musician, although I personally think that being able to improvise, and play "by ear" is at *least* as important a skill. However, "reading" (as musicians call it) does allow us to learn any song that any other musician has written down, which makes a tremendous amount of material (mostly classical and jazz) available. It's certainly well worth knowing the basics of reading, even if you don't choose to pursue it further at present. And it does take some pursuing, and some practice, since learning standard notation is rather like learning to read a foreign language — quite a bit of memorization, and lots of new rules that don't seem to make sense.

If you've read the previous music theory appendix (and if you haven't, you'd better), you know that each note has a letter name, and some notes have two (a sharp name # and a flat name b). In standard notation, instead of indicating a specific note with a letter, we indicate a specific note by its position on a set of lines and spaces called a **staff**.

There are two kinds of staffs used. One, called the **bass staff** or **lower staff**, is for writing down low notes. The other is called a **treble staff** or **upper staff**, and it's used for writing down higher notes. You can tell what kind of staff you're looking at by the symbol called a bass clef (pictured at left) or a treble clef (pictured at right) at the beginning of the staff. Most harmonica music is written on the treble staff, although the lowest notes of the sixteen hole harps could also be written on the bass staff.

Even the eight hole chromatics have too many notes to fit on the five lines and four spaces of the treble clef. So musicians add extra lines called **leger lines** above and below the staff, to put the higher and lower notes on.

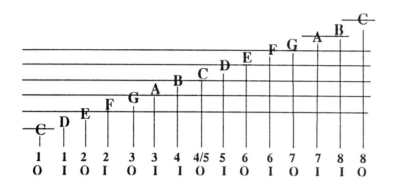

1	1	2	2	3	3	4	4/5	5	6	6	7	7	8	8
O	I	O	I	O	I	I	O	I	O	I	O	I	I	O

Here are the In and Out notes of holes 1 to 8 without using the slide. These, of course, are the notes used to play the C Major Scale. Practice playing your C Major Scales from holes 1 to 8 while looking at the letter names of the notes on the staff, from left to right.

It's inconvenient and hard to read if we to put too many leger lines above the staff when writing the highest notes (like the 9 to 12 holes) of a twelve or sixteen hole chro. Instead, when writing these high notes down, we write the letters *8va* followed by a dotted line that extends over the high notes we're writing. Then we write the 9 to 12 hole notes *as though* they were 5 to 8 hole notes.

We do the same thing with the low 1 to 4 notes of the sixteen holer, except that we write *sub8* under them, and then write them *as though* they were regular 1 to 4 notes.

If you want to read, you'll need to memorize where these notes fall. Some notes are easy to remember. For instance, the note E (2 Out) is the note on the bottom line, the note C (1 Out) is the note on the first leger line under the staff, and the note F (6 In) is the note on the top line of the staff. Some people like to try to memorize the notes by using the sentence **Every Good Boy Does Fine** to remember the notes on the lines, and the word **F-A-C-E** to remember the notes on the spaces between the notes.

Reading standard notation is a two part process. We must learn the letter names of the notes that our chro can produce, and we must learn where these notes fall on the staff. Spend some time looking at the above chart while slowly playing the C Major Scales from 1 to 4 and 5 to 8. After a while, try to look only at the letter names on the staff, and not at the hole notation at the bottom.

Standard Rhythm Notation

You're almost ready to begin reading simple songs, since you know which note is represented by which line and space. All you need is to know how long to hold each note.

Instead of placing letter names on the lines and spaces of the staff, as I did above, in standard musical notation note symbols are used to represent notes. The main part of the note, which looks like a small oval, will be centered on a particular line or space to let you know which note to play. And the shading of the oval part (black or white), and the type of **stem** attached to it will tell you how long to play it for.

A **whole note** tells you to hold a note for four complete beats. It isn't used too commonly. A **half note** tells you to hold a note for two beats. A **quarter note** has a *stem*, and tells you to hold the note for one beat. It's probably the most often used note. By the way, it doesn't matter whether the stem points up or down. The **eighth note** has a *flag,*

Whole = 4 beats   Half = 2 beats   Quarter = 1 beat   Eighth = 1/2 beat   Sixteenth = 1/4 beat

and tells you to hold the note for half a beat. When two or more eighth notes occur in a row, they can be written with a single flag connecting them, called a *beam*. A **sixteenth note** has two flags, and tells you to hold a note for just a quarter beat.

Sometimes, just as I've indicated beats of silence by placing dots without hole numbers under them, standard notation tells you not to play anything for a while. It does this by placing **rests** on the staff. The **quarter rests** tell you not to play for one beat. The **half rest** tells you not to play for two beats. The **whole rest** tells you not to play for four beats, and the **eighth rest** tells you not to play for only half a beat. If the music requires silence for an amount of time other than these, you'll see more than one rest. For instance, a three beat rest would be indicated by showing a half rest (two beats) and a quarter rest (one beat).

Whole rest = 4 beats   Half = 2 beats   Quarter = 1 beat   Eighth = 1/2 beat

Bar lines break up the music into bars (useful for us twelve bar blues fans). Most of the music that we play has four beats to each bar, but some music (like waltzes, or certain country tunes) has three beats to the bar. At the beginning of every song, we will see a **time signature** composed of two numbers, one over the other. The top number will tell us how many beats are in each bar, almost always either three or four. The bottom number will tell us what type of note gets one beat. This number will usually be a 4, since the quarter note usually represents one beat. In some jazz and blues music, the composer writes the music so that one beat is represented by an eighth note instead of a quarter note, but this is not too common.

Practice playing this bouncy C Major Scale, written with quarter and eighth notes. Use a "dirty" or "dada" articulation to break one beat into two parts for the eighth notes. Then try a simple version of Frankie and Johnny (the same as the one on page 61).

Swingin' the Beat

As you remember, in most blues music we swing the beat, that is, when a single beat is divided into two parts, we hold the first one a bit longer instead of making them both equal. In standard notation, we place a **dot** after a note to indicate that the note should be held for half again as long as we usually would hold it. So, a half note (usually two beats long) with a dot would be held for three beats, a quarter note (usually one beat long) with a dot would be held for one and a half beats, and an eighth note (usually half a beat long) with a dot would be held for three-quarters of a beat. These notes are called **dotted halves, dotted quarters,** and **dotted eighths.**

The standard way of indicating a swing beat is to write it using a dotted eighth note and a sixteenth note, tied together with a beam. This tells us that the two notes share one beat, but the first note should be held for three-quarters of a beat, and the second note should be held for one-quarter of a beat.

Playing in Keys Other than C

Reading in the key of C Major, which means using the notes of the C Major Scale, is pretty easy. There are no sharp or flat notes in C Major. But as soon as we try to read in any other key, we need to learn how to read sharps and flats. As when writing down note names, sharps and flats in standard notation are represented by # and b signs. The sharp or flat sign is placed in front of the note, so that you can tell before you play the note whether it needs to be sharped or flatted.

Reading then playing sharps is easy. Whenever you see a # in front of a note, just remember the letter name of the note, locate it on the chro, and push the slide in on that note. Flats are harder, since you need to memorize which note is *above* the one that you have to push the slide in on. Forget flats for now, and try playing this C Blues Scale, with its three sharped (slide pressed in) notes. I've thrown in one expanded Blues Scale note (the 3 In), and a bit of swing rhythm, to make it more fun.

Usually, when writing standard notation in a non C Major key, the writers expect to be using sharps or flats on certain notes throughout the song. For instance, if we were writing a song that uses the E Major Scale for most of its notes, we would expect the notes F#, G#, C#, and D# to occur quite often, since they are E Major Scale notes (see page 96 if you don't believe me. So we would begin our song with a **key signature,** which is one or more sharp or flat signs next to the treble clef, on particular lines or spaces. The key signature tells us that all or most of the notes on the lines or spaces with key signature sharps or flats on them will be sharped or flatted *throughout* that song.

If for some reason the composer decides that one of the notes that usually is sharped or flatted *shouldn't* be, that note will be preceded by a natural sign (pictured at left). A natural sign usually refers not only to the note in front of which it is placed, but also to any other notes of that type in the same bar. When the bar is over, the note is again meant to be sharped or flatted, unless it has another natural sign. So in the following example of an E Major lick with a few E Blues Scale notes, in the first and third bars the notes on the G and D lines are sharped (we know that because the key signature has # signs on the G and D lines). In the second and fourth bars the notes on the G and D lines aren't sharped, to give us some E Blues Scale notes (we know this because of the natural signs in front of the G and D notes.

By the way, sharps or flats in a key signature tell you to sharpen or flatten all notes with the same letter name as the letter name that the key signature sharps or flats are on. So if you see a key signature sharp sign on the top line of the staff (an F note), you must also sharpen any *lower f* note that you see on the bottom space of the staff.

If this all seems somewhat complex, I agree! If you would like more help with the rhythm aspects of reading, our *Instant Rhythm Kit* will do just that. And if you need some more help with reading in general, try Howard Shanet's *Learn to Read Music*, from Simon & Schuster. Buy a beginner's songbook for any instrument in the key of C, and just practice it some, without being self-critical.

Appendix B: Accompaniment

If you have a friend who plays even minimal guitar or keyboard, you can have a wonderful time playing together. Simply have them play a repeated C chord while you follow the instructions for the C Blues Jamm. They can also play a D minor chord for all your D Jamm work (pages 33 to 45). Record a few minutes of their playing so that you can work out on your own,.

If you don't know someone who can do that, you can provide *yourself* with some good C backing. Just use a cassette deck, and record yourself playing a few minutes of the basic Dirty Dirty Dog pattern as described on page 28. Then play it back, and jamm along using the variety of C jamm techniques from pages 27 to 31. Do the same thing for your D Jamms by recording a few minutes of simple Dirty Dirty Dogs on the 1, 2, and 3 In notes (which provide a D minor chord), then playing them back and jamming with them.

Show your accompanist my description of the basic 12 Bar Blues in C and D on page 51, and they should be able to knock out a few verses for you to play along with. Or, after you've learned to play these yourself, record some verses of the basic C and D 12 Bar Blues on your chro, and then use it as backing when you learn some of the fancier licks and jamms that go along with it!

Appendix C: The Bigger Chros

You've probably noticed that many of the songs and licks use mostly the notes from holes 1 to 8. This is for two reasons. Firstly, because I know that every one of my readers has at least that many notes to play with. And secondly, because the 9 to 12 hole range is higher than many people prefer to listen to for very long.

But if you've got a big chro, and would like to be able to play some of the lower licks on your higher end, the following chart will tell you which notes are the same. Simply take the low end lick (say a 2 In - 3 Out - 4 In combo) that you want to translate into a high end lick, and see which notes in the high end are the same as that 2 In, that 3 Out, and that 4 In. Looking directly beneath the 2 In, 3 Out, and 4 In, we see that 6 In, 7 Out, and 8 In provide the same F - G - B notes, as do 10 In, 11 Out, and 12 In. Get the idea?

By the way, most 16 holers do not have holes 12 to 16 marked. Instead, the first four holes are numbered 1 to 4, but with a little dot over each number. These extra low notes are exactly the same as the 1-4 of an eight or twelve holer, only lower sounding. The next twelve holes of the biggest chros are numbered 1 through 12.

C	C#	D	D#	E	F	F	F#	G	G#	A	A#	B	C	C(D)	C#
1	1	1	1	2	2	2	2	3	3	3	3	4	4	4	4
O	◎	I	◖	O	◎	I	◖	O	◎	I	◖	I	O	◖	◎

5	5	5	5	6	6	6	6	7	7	7	7	8	8	8*	8
O	◎	I	◖	O	◎	I	◖	O	◎	I	◖	I	O	◖	◎

9	9	9	9	10	10	10	10	11	11	11	11	12	12	12*	12
O	◎	I	◖	O	◎	I	◖	O	◎	I	◖	I	O	◖	◎

* Note: Whether you have an eight, twelve, or sixteen hole chromatic, the notes of the *highest* hole of your instrument will be arranged slightly differently than you'd expect. In an eight holer, the 8 In slide note provides a D rather than the C that you would expect from looking at the 4 hole. It's the same with hole 12 of a twelve holer, and the highest hole of a sixteen holer. It actually makes sense, if you think about it, because that extra C would be less useful than the D (which is not otherwise available up there and which allows you to get one higher note out of the harp)!

More Good Stuff from David Harp

Instant Blues Harmonica!

If you like chromatic harmonica, you'll probably love the ten hole diatonic harp. It's excitingly different from the chro — inexpensive, easy to carry in a pocket — every chro player should double on the blues harp! Our package for ten hole is in its seventh complete revision, and way over 100,000 people have already used it. Book, 90 minute tape, and high quality Huang Silvertone Deluxe harmonica (key of C) only $19.95 ($12.95 without harp).

Instant Blues and Rock Harmonica: The Video

It's probably the easiest way to learn to blow your blues away — a 60 minute Video Tape for beginning blues harmonica players! Created for Arlen Roth's Hot Licks Video series, with superb production values. If you want to learn blues harp fastest, this is the way to go. $49.95 includes high quality Huang Star Performer harmonica (Key of G).

Instant Chromatic Harmonica: The Cassette

If you've made it this far, you already know all about the tape. It's 90 minutes long, illustrates the material in the book, and has lots of good play-along songs. Only $9.95.

Bending The Blues

An entire 64 page book and 90 minute cassette devoted entirely to bending! Everything you could possibly want to know, from how to get that first faint bend, to breaking the 3 hole into five useable notes, and overblowing the 4, 5, and 6 Out holes. All draw and blow bends explained and demonstrated in tremendous detail. If you play ten hole harp, this will add 16 extra notes to the 20 you've got! Although not created for the chromatic harp, a few hours of practice with this and a ten hole harmonica will improve your chro bending skills more than you might believe. Only $12.95 ($19.95 with Huang Silvertone).

Instant Rhythm Kit

Rhythm is the heartbeat of all music, and this book, cassette, and custom beginner drumstick set will help you to develop a great sense of rhythm — even if you don't think you have one at all! Whether you're a would-be drummer, or you don't know a rock backbeat from a jazz triplet or a blues shuffle, this package is for you. Includes rock, blues, jazz, Latin and African rhythms, solos, fills, and much more. Unless you're already a good percussionist, this book can't help but improve your musicianship — on any instrument! Only $16.95.

Instant Guitar for the Musical Idiot!

Play guitar chords using only one finger! This package is like nothing you've ever seen or tried before! Strictly for *absolute, total beginners* who can't play at all! Not for serious students, but perfect for kids, parents, teachers, scout leaders — anybody who'd like to play a bit of Folk, Blues, Country, Classical, Jazz or "New Age" music within minutes! 80 page Book, 98 minute tape, and amazingly simple invention, "The ChordSnaffle", only $14.95.

Instant Flute!

This entertaining package will teach you to play Folk, Blues, Classical, Country, and Traditional Irish music right away! Over 70 songs, including *Greensleeves, Amazing Grace, Saint Jame's Infirmary Blues, House of the Rising Sun, Beethoven's Ninth, John Barleycorn,* and *John Henry.* Special section on Blues /Jazz improvisation, Christmas Carols, Fiddle Tunes, Traditional Irish and English Music. The package includes a 64 page book and top quality block flute (flageolet, tinwhistle) from Britain. Try it! A wonderful gift for ages 8-98, only $14.95.

Instant Harmonica For Kids!

Give a child the lifelong gift of music! It's a great music education for ages 4 - 9, combining my decades of teaching experience with techniques selected from the Yamaha, Suzuki, and Orff-Schulwerk methods of childhood musical education. They'll learn while having loads of fun! 64 page book, 90 minute cassette, and high quality harp only $19.95.

Our fine products are available in better music stores, or order them direct from:

musical i press

RD # 3   Box 3400 - C   Middlesex, Vermont 05602

Phone Orders (802) 223 - 1544
Fax Orders (802) 223 - 0543
Visa and Mastercharge welcome

To order, call us or send a **check or money order** (and clearly identify each of the items you want). Please also include the following **Shipping & Handling** charges (we ship via UPS unless otherwise requested):

U.S. orders: Add $3.00 for first item, $1.00 each additional item. Orders over $50.00 shipped free!
C.O.D. Orders (U.S. only) add additional $3.50 for UPS C.O.D. Charges.

Canadian Orders: Add $4.00 for first item, $2.00 each additional item. Orders over $75.00 shipped free!

Other Foreign orders: Please add $6.00 per item.

Volume discounts available on all items. Please call or write for details.